"GRANDY, LET'S PLAY!"

"GRANDY, LET'S PLAY!"

Reflections on the Joy, Blessings,
and Wonder of Grandparenting

ANDY BECKER

"Grandy, Let's Play!"
Reflections on the Joy, Blessings, and Wonder of Grandparenting
The Spirtual Garden Series

Andy Becker

Published by Tree of the Field Publishing
http://www.andybecker.life/

TREE OF THE FIELD
—— PUBLISHING ——

ISBN: 978-1-7336698-3-2

Illustrations by Abigail Drapkin

**The complete *Spiritual Garden Series*
by Andy Becker**

The Spiritual Gardener:
Insights from the Jewish Tradition to Help
Your Garden Grow (Second Edition)

The Spiritual Forest:
Timeless Jewish Wisdom for a Healthier Planet
and a Richer Spiritual Life

"Grandy, Let's Play!"
Reflections on the Joy, Blessings, and
Wonder of Grandparenting

To my family and to grandparents everywhere.

CONTENTS

INTRODUCTION

"May you live to see your children's children—
peace be on Israel."
PSALM 128:6

The overarching themes of my three books in the *Spiritual Garden Series* are broadly drawn from the teachings of Jewish mysticism; we should live with joy, inspiration, and purpose. Satisfaction and living an authentic life springs from awareness of the beauty that surrounds us in the garden, in the forest, and perhaps most of all, in the bosom of our families. In this book, a collection of stand-alone stories that reflect on grandparenting, I hope to convey that way of looking at things.

As a grandparent, you get to reinvent yourself a bit with babies and toddlers who have no preconceived idea of you. You may alter your own self-concept, if you so desire. Why not let the next generation experience you as you want to be, radiating life, humor, and energy? You have a chance to be in the moment, unrushed, engaged, and fulfilled. You have a built-in opportunity in the family hierarchy to model all the positive attributes that you want the grandchildren to eventually acquire: patience, thoughtfulness, generosity, and kindness.

Parents of babies and toddlers, especially working parents, are stretched thin. If you are able to help them out, not reluctantly but enthusiastically, you are bringing your family closer together while benefiting everyone, including yourself. You are a calming reassurance and support to the parents who may struggle with childcare. They know the baby or toddler is safe, secure, and loved in your care.

The baby hits the jackpot with grandparents. She gets all the love, stimulation, and attention a grandparent is happy to provide. The grandparent gets to relive the joy of a newborn baby or toddler without the stresses of a first-time parent trying to figure out how to care for one. Babysitting or visiting grandchildren provides countless hours of entertainment, more captivating than anything on a television screen, and it's commercial-free.

Whether articulated or intuited, grandparenting is a profound spiritual blessing. The bilateral discoveries during a baby and young toddler's rapid development are often spontaneous and surprising, soul-opening and inspiring. The greatest revelation of all might be that special connection a focused grandparent can provide. The energy usually flows both ways, with humor and joy, and is clearly reinvigorating for the older human in this relationship. The younger human eats up the attention.

I wrote *The Spiritual Gardener* to encourage home gardening. I wrote *The Spiritual Forest* to promote an environmental ethic from a spiritual perspective. *Grandy, Let's Play!* is intended to share the elation of having grandchildren and the joys of spending time with them.

Jews often say to each other, especially when drinking a toast on an auspicious occasion, "L'chaim!"—which means "To life!" Chai, in Hebrew, is the word for life. In Jewish mysticism, the word Chai also has a numeric value of eighteen, which is considered a very lucky number. This is why Jews traditionally give charity and gifts in multiples of eighteen. It is not a coincidence that each book in the *Spiritual Garden Series* has eighteen chapters, stories drawn from my life experiences. I have been extremely lucky in my life, especially with regard to my family.

I hope some of my luck shines through in The *Spiritual Garden Series* and rubs off on you when you read, *Grandy, Let's Play!* L'chaim!

GRANDY

(The Blessing of a Daughter-in-Law)

"A daughter-in-law is like a bonus daughter—
double the love, double the fun!"
MARK TWAIN

Families often come up with special pet names for the grandparents. Mine is Grandy. I was bestowed the name Grandy by my beautiful daughter-in-law, who, by the way, often no longer calls me by my first name, Andy, but now calls me Grandy. The grandparent does not pick a new name; a member of the family does. If it's a good choice, everyone in the family uses it, and the old name is replaced.

My sister was the first-born in my nuclear family and the first grandchild. She nicknamed my grandfather, whose name was Joseph, I-I, pronounced aye-aye. The genesis for this was a song he sang to her when she was a baby that went, "Aye, yi, yi, yi." The name stuck for all the succeeding grandchildren. His actual name was Yusef, which is Joseph in English. He went by Joe, but I never heard him called Joe unless it was followed by his last name, Goldberg; so, it was always Joe Goldberg in one breath.

In Joe Goldberg's case, his very close friends and some family members also called him a loving Yiddish nickname, Yussel, or Yussele, the diminutive of Yussel. But to his grandchildren, he was always and only I-I. Of course, in ancient times, Jews didn't have surnames, but rather were named with their own names and their father's name, e.g., Yusef ben Yitzak (Joseph, son of Isacc).

My parents named me Andrew, which means manly and brave, apparently a popular biblical name in Judea during the first century. I never knew Andrew meant manly and brave, two qualities that probably don't immediately come to mind when I or others think of me—or, at the very least, when I think of myself. I was surprised by the meanings when I first looked up the origin of the name in adulthood. As a kid, I never knew names had some sort of original meanings or histories. I don't think missing this knowledge in childhood affected my self-concept. In any event, no one familiar with me ever called me Andrew. I've always been Andy.

My brother, Stephen, was Stevie, and my sister, Deborah, was Debbie. My children, Matthew and Samuel, were mostly Matt and Sam, never a Matty, but often a Sammy. My daughter-in-law is Karly. Her older siblings are Kristy and Kevin. I don't know why they all have K names, but they get along marvelously, and they each reflect distinctive qualities, more decidedly influenced by genetics, parenting, and birth order than the shared first letter of their names.

Some names, like my wife's first name, have a backstory. Her dad was expecting his first child to be a boy that he would name after an older brother, lionized by the family, who was lost in World War II. When the baby was a girl, he had to pivot. His name was Donald, and his wife's name was Ruth, so the baby became Donna Ruth.

According to *Wikipedia*, the name Donna originated from Italian and means "lady" or "woman." It derives from the Latin word "*domina*," which has the same meaning. This name has historically been associated with elegance, grace, and strength, all qualities my wife Donna possesses. Donna, however, never liked the name and fantasized as a prepubescent about calling herself Brooke. She romanticized that name, writing it over and over in a notebook and imagining herself as a pop singer.

Some Jewish names are taken from animals. For example, Judah is a lion. Yonah means dove, and Rachel means ewe. Deborah, my sister's name, is the Hebrew name for bee, which I find amusing because she never resembled anything bee-like.

In a perfect world, a name would match one's identity, but a name is usually chosen before a baby's personality is clearly demonstrated to the parents doing the naming. Parents usually settle on a name even before the birthing.[1] If they're smart, they keep the baby's name to themselves to avoid a lot of unwelcome kibbitzing, especially from family members, like soon-to-be grandparents, whose own grandparent nicknames are yet to be determined. In fact, grandparent nicknames aren't even on anyone's radar in the early days of infancy. During the final dog days of pregnancy, especially with a firstborn, the expectant parents' focus is much broader than the baby's name. There's a lot on their plate.

When it comes to the flip side, what the first-born baby is going to call the grandparents, the new addition to the family is often calling the shots, like my sister calling my grandfather I-I. We might be familiar with common nicknames like grandma, grandpa, granddad, pop-pop, nana, papa, maw-maw and pawpaw, grams and gramps, grammy and grampie, and the Yiddish bubbe or bubbeleh—names that were convenient for the baby to repeat.

---

1   This is not universal. According to Wiki, some Native American cultures name and rename family members based on experences and characteristics that develop later in life.

In my case, in a genius moment, my daughter-in-law spontaneously told my grandson that my name was Grandy. Thus, my daughter-in-law preempted the baby, but I instantly took to the name. As a combo of Andy and Grandpa, it immediately felt very natural to be called Grandy. This happened long before our precious first-born grandchild was speaking words that we could make out and while he was still cooing and bubbling. At the time, I was holding the baby, and he was giving me a very taciturn look. Maybe his expression conveyed to Mom that he was thinking, "Who is this guy?" and Mom was simply answering the question. His expression didn't change upon hearing Grandy's name for the first time, but Grandy's did.

I don't know of any other Grandys, so the name feels wonderfully unique and special to me. Grand means magnificent and impressive, like a grand staircase, ballroom, or piano, so the name also feels highly complimentary.

Nothing is sweeter to my ears when we walk in the door for a visit than, "Grandy play cars!" or on a video phone call, "Where's Grandy? I wanna see Grandy!"

Now, if I was called something else, like Grandpa, Grandpa Andy, or Papa Andy, I'd be just as happy hearing those words. I'm not claiming victory over all the other grandfathers of the world because my daughter-in-law named me Grandy. I just really like being called Grandy.

In the world of jokes and proverbs, there are plenty of nasty ones about the difficulties between a mother or father-in-law vis-à-vis a daughter-in-law. I don't know if they are an outgrowth of longstanding cultural misogyny or some other historical examples of how we put down women in society. I don't understand that kind of humor.

The fact is that your daughter-in-law carried, birthed, and suckled your grandchild. She connects to that child in beautiful ways that you never will. You are never going to feel anything but love and gratitude when she hands you her baby to hold. Same with dad. And although "Da-da" might be the greatest dad ever, "Mama" is always going to be the child's first choice, the number one preference, clearly the best and most important person in the universe. She deserves nothing but love, respect, and care from her in-laws, the grandparents.

It is beyond argument that being a grandparent is a tremendous blessing in and of itself. For my daughter-in-law to bestow upon me the name of Grandy is surely a wonderful and cherished bonus. The name stuck. What a gift, thank you! Has it changed my identity or impacted my self-concept? Perhaps not when I'm out and about, but when I'm with my grandchildren, I am 100 percent Grandy—and I am 100 percent blessed.

IDEAS

- *Does your daughter-in-law like chocolate? How about bringing her a small box on your next visit?*

- *Ask if there is any interest in planning a joint family vacation or a fun day trip.*

- *Book a pedicure with your daughter-in-law.*

BEEP-BEEP

(The Value of Play)

"The quality of a cucumber can be recognized
when it is still a blossom."
—TALMUD, BERACHOT: 48A

My wife saved some of our kids' favorite books and toys from when they were small fry. Some of the stuff we should have given away, but some things she couldn't part with. Those included a brand of stuffed animals called Beanie Babies, Pokémon cards, a Brio train set, artwork, and prized schoolwork, dating all the way back to their Montessori preschool days and up through high school. It's amazing how quickly feelings well up after all these years from seeing physical objects that evoke memories of times our children spent under our roof.

The kids weren't that old when we moved into a house that had a big basement closet with a bunch of shelves. The more shelves, the more stuff that never goes away. That is the way it is. We promised ourselves we'd go through what was stored there when we moved in, but we never did; in fact, we used the space to randomly store many more things. Soon, we will enter our third decade in this same abode. The kids have lived independently for well over a decade. A lot of kid stuff sat in boxes and containers in this large closet, preserved but unused, and almost completely out of mind—until we had grandchildren.

Once we had grandchildren, it was time to rummage around in the basement closet. Was there anything there a grandchild might enjoy? We kept so many books, including some really good ones. We found the giant container of Beanie Babies. We knew we'd find the Brio train set with its wooden trains, tracks, and bridges. There were some wooden puzzles and puppets. And we found an entire shoe box of Matchbox and Hot Wheel cars, some well-worn, but most looking good if not in mint condition.

When Eon, our first grandchild, was about a year and a half, we saw that he liked cars. I started bringing a few cars every visit. Although Eon was already excited when Grandma Donna and I came by, who doesn't like a little present? Letting Eon unwrap each of his grandparents' hands to discover two new cars added to his excitement.

To frequently give a little kid a gift is neither a bribe nor a reward. A bribe is offered, often in desperation, to seek a child's cooperation under difficult circumstances. Bribery also connotes unethical behavior and, in fact, is discouraged in parenting. A reward is subtly different than a bribe. A reward is an offer in advance, structured to motivate a behavior. A bribe is often offered after the offending behavior in a weak attempt to cut it off. Grandparents are wise to leave the rewards and bribes to the parents and focus on just giving.

We gave Eon the cars without any strings attached. We discovered an unused box of them, and he was thrilled to have them. Why should they sit unused on a shelf? We gave them out two at a time so as to not overwhelm. What grandparents don't want to see their grandchild beam with joy?

"Let's play cars!" Eon told us as he ran from the front door with his "new" cars to the family room/play area right off the kitchen. There, his other cars were parked in a line on a shelf that he could easily reach. "Hi, I'm Po-Po," he said, holding his police car. "Hi, I'm Number 9, Speed Racer," I replied, grabbing a hotrod. "Beep-beep-beep," backed up Po-Po. "Beep-beep-beep," backed up Number 9 Speed Racer next to Po-Po.

Sometimes, Eon liked to run a car up and down our arms or legs. Sometimes, a grandparent's arm served as a runway for the cars to fly off to different places until they landed on the sofa. Sometimes, the pillows or the back of the couch were big hills that were hard to drive up. Other times, the crack between the sofa cushions served as a gas station.

Eon's play wasn't only about the cars. It was about the undivided attention he enjoyed from us. Little cars are that much more fun when you get to play and laugh with your grandparents on the sofa or on the floor. When Mom and Dad came home from work, they always shared Eon's excitement when he showed them that day's two new cars, if they weren't temporarily lost, buried in the sofa. We can thank Grandma Donna, for saving that old shoebox full of little cars.

Over time, there were a lot of cars. The play usually started with a conversation between cars, often with a simple, "Hi." Many cars had names, like School Bus, España Tour Bus, Big Trucky, Pickup Truck, Sedan Racer, Dodge Challenger, Jaguar, Corvette, Jeep-jeep, Chevy, and Rover 500. We used a stack of books to make a ramp. The cars shot down the ramp, colliding one into another, one by one. Sometimes, Eon liked to hide the cars on the sofa under a pillow or drive them up the side of the couch and down again, sometimes crashing them on the floor. We played with the cars so much that Eon's parents, Grandma Donna, and I all remembered their different names.

Several of the cars had doors, hoods, or trunks that opened and closed, which took a lot of hand-eye coordination. The car crashing stopped momentarily as Eon carefully opened and closed the parts on some of the cars that had moving parts. Playing cars with Eon gave us more than a taste of his ability to concentrate, explore, pretend, and create. His attention span was very good. His personality, charming and engaging, was what we loved most.

Playing cars became so popular that Eon's Dad bought a long toy ramp with two lanes that worked great for racing cars. It had sections that clipped together. With all the pieces affixed, the ramp extended across half the room. Eon needed a little help to fit the pieces together to build the ramp. We raced pairs of cars over and over. Sometimes, they smashed into the cars that sat at the bottom of the ramp.

When it was time for lunch, Grandma Donna suggested that we first put away the toys. Eon demonstrated his toddler capacity to organize, as sports cars went in one area, the construction cars in another. The special cars, like the ambulance and the school bus, were lined up with each other.

Eon had a special song for putting away his toys. It went like this:

Clean up, clean up,
Everybody, everywhere.

Clean up, clean up,
Everybody, do your share.

Clean up, clean up.
Everybody, clean up.

Time to clean up, everybody!

We were happy to help pick up the cars and the other toys that went on the shelves. Grandma Donna and I sang along with Eon. It usually took only a minute when everyone joined in.

IDEAS

- *Have you ever invited your toddler to a tea party? Perhaps, a favorite stuffed animal or two might like to attend and eat some imaginary cookies.*

- *Is it raining outside? How about a dance party? Does your toddler have a favorite song?*

- *Still raining? Make a collage with stickers and crayons or a craft item together.*

- *Is it nice outside? Time to go for a walk to the playground!*

GIZMOS

(Adapting to Technology)

"A righteous man falls down seven times and gets up."
PROVERBS 24:16

Security Cameras. "Smile, you're on *Candid Camera*!" If you grew up in the sixties, you may remember this television program—secret cameras filmed innocent victims put in precarious situations. The point of the show was to laugh at their expense. The more foolish the reaction, the funnier, or so thought the show's producers.

Surveillance cameras are now ubiquitous to monitor your doorbell, your pets—or your nanny. Do you want a cordless gizmo with rechargeable batteries or a plug-in? Do you need one that is weather-resistant for outside mounting, with or without blinding spotlights? How about 180-degree views? Do you pay for a memory card, or do you prefer a subscription service?

Of course, the behemoth Amazon created the wonderful convenience of front-door delivery ("free" with Prime). It did not take long for thieves to discover package pilfering (*Gonefs benei gonefs!*—Thieves, sons of thieves!) Clearly, this exploded the market for security cameras. Are you at the office, job site, or on the road? No problem. You now can view, in real time, who just rang your doorbell on your phone or desktop. And let's not forget the goal of deterring terrorists that justify public cameras on city streets. It is only a matter of time until everyone will be able to see everything at all times, thanks to a network of cameras mounted on walls and street lamps, in computers and phones, and in the sky on satellites and drones.

What conscientious, modern parents wouldn't want to monitor their precious babies, asleep in the crib, at the daycare, or with the babysitter, in real time on their smartphones or desktops at work? While we thought only God, the blessed Holy One, was omnipresent, it turns out so are the baby's parents. Conditioned to screens with alerts for meetings, driving directions, how-to YouTubes, games, and a million apps, today's parents of newborns quickly adopt a whole range of new screen-friendly technologies.

What does this mean for the new grandparents? Although you are likely the most trusted people in the entire universe to babysit, you, too, are being surveilled and recorded. All the goofy faces and sounds you make babysitting the precious newborn are now recorded for all time. True, no contemporary parent has the time to assemble your most embarrassing grandparent goofball moments into a video collage or blog, but the fact remains that "big brother" may be watching at any time.

This is unlikely to change your behavior. You have lived to hold a grandchild in your arms. You don't care if you are on *Candid Camera* or if anyone is watching. This is an inestimable, unquantifiable, cherished time.

You hold the little fingers, you smile and coo, and before long, the baby coos back to the smiles and coo ki-choos. You sing about the itsy-bitsy spider. You hold the baby up to the window to look at the rain and the cars rolling by. You have a baby in your arms. Together, you explore the world.

Strollers. At some point, ready or not, God help you, it is time to leave the house. We know, at least from the time of the Pharaohs, parents were putting babies in baskets. Moses was put in a basket coated with pitch and floated down a marshy part of the Nile. History records children being carried in slings and backpacks by many indigenous cultures. Swaddled onto a cradleboard, many a baby felt warm and secure on the back of a parent, typically Mom. That freed the adult hands to attend to daily tasks, while keeping the baby's hands wrapped up and out of trouble. Cradles, baskets, and bassinets were also means to carry infants from one spot to the next. But when did we start putting wheels on the baskets?

The first baby carriages in the 1700s belonged to English nobility—kings, queens, dukes, and the like. They were highly decorated baskets on wheels that the privileged offspring could sit in while being pulled by a goat or a pony. It wasn't long before Americans in the 1800s made standard models that included brakes and umbrellas that a parent or nanny could push around.

William H. Richardson, an African American, patented his idea of the first reversible stroller in 1889. His design allowed each wheel to move separately, increasing maneuverability. Fast forward to the 1960s. An aeronautical engineer designed an umbrella stroller with an aluminum frame, and soon, strollers gained widespread popularity around the globe.[2]

---

2 Wikipedia contributors, "Baby transport," Wikipedia, The Free Encyclopedia, https://en.wikipedia.org/w/index.php?title=Baby_transport&oldid=1241442461 (accessed September 22, 2024).

Today, strollers are just as, if not more, numerous than security cameras. We have full-size strollers, travel strollers, jogging strollers, and double strollers. By the time the grandparents have learned how to work the firstborn's stroller, baby brother is welcoming a new baby sister into the family. Oy vey, it's time for a double stroller! For the grandparent, this means it's time to reenroll in Stroller University. The only problem is there is no Stroller U, no Stroller State College, and no Stroller Community College. Hopefully, the parents will ease the grandparents into their new double-stroller experiences by letting them watch the unfolding and correct adjustments of the contraption while strapping the right babies into the right compartments. The grandparent's initial job is limited to pushing the stroller and applying and releasing the foot break at the crosswalks. This simple action involves detailed instructions and vigilance by the newborn's conscientious parents.

But time marches on. At some point, it is reasonable for the parents to assume that you watched the folding and unfolding, the strapping in, and the unbuckling enough times that you have achieved stroller competency. But when a parent is no longer around to help, the rubber hits the sidewalk.

The first challenge is unfolding the stroller, which is surprisingly much harder than unfolding those difficult lawn chairs at home. It goes something like this: It's locked. I can unlock it, somehow. Hmmm, that didn't work. How to unlock the lock? Okay, I'm pressing a button, but nothing is happening. Ah, wrong button. Maybe this is the right button? If I only had a third arm and hand, I could try to pull this bottom part with the big wheels out while pressing these two side buttons. Oh, look at this, you just have to hold the handle and give it a flop. I wish I'd tried that before all these isometric exercises and back strains.

While the darn thing is now unfolded, let's lock the brakes to click in the car seat parts that are lying there on the floor. Okay, this seat installs in the back, facing back, but what about the top seat? Does it face forward or backward? Wait a minute, which is the upper seat and which is the lower? They look a little different in size. *Oy vey es meir.* (Woe is me.) You simply can't remember which one goes exactly where, and which way is which. Now you are perspiring. You are so stressed out you have to go to the bathroom.

Logic dictates that the upper seat is the smaller one. But if that's so, why is it going to squish down and compromise the room available for the bottom seat? Turn it around? Oh no, here are the adapter spacers that raise it up higher, so there's room in the bottom one for an actual human being rather than just the diaper bag. (A modern diaper bag is a backpack filled with various compartments, including wipes and diapers on one side and snacks, bibs, and silicone plates on the other. Make sure, before you go out, that it has the diapers!)

Finally, the stroller looks correctly assembled. Uppy-up, let's lift the child in without banging any heads, legs, or feet, at least not bad enough to cause a concussion, sprain, or an arm pulled out of a socket. Once your patient grandchildren are finally sitting in the stroller, you fiddle with the seat belts and shoulder straps. Why are they so impossibly tight? Why don't the arm straps click into the seat belt? Here we go—click. But wait a minute! This is way too tight! This cannot be comfortable. How the . . . (don't say it in front of your grandkids) do you loosen this strap?! Under no circumstances can you use the invectives you spontaneously spout when things don't fit. It turns out the reason the shoulder straps won't click in is because there's a button under the gizmo that clicks. You are supposed to loosen it up before clicking and *then* do the tightening.

You have to pull down the seat's Velcro back to adjust the shoulder straps! Does this mean we need to take the kiddies out and start from scratch? *Oy gevalt*! Is this being recorded on a surveillance video? After more fumbling and bumbling, somehow, someway, two little kids are hooked in and ready for a ride to the park. The baby is in the carriage facing you, while her big brother is enjoying the view from the front, facing forwards.

About halfway there, the big brother decides he wants out. Since there are two grandparents, it's not a problem if he wants to walk, but that's not what he wants. He wants to ride from behind. *He* shows *you* how to fold down a little platform so that he can stand on it and face baby sister. This is ingenious. If he were to fall back somehow, which he won't, but if he did, you are there to catch him. Let's go, with the little guy standing and holding on.

Baby instantly smiles, looking at her big brother, who is repositioned on the back platform. Big brother bends his knees and burrows his head into baby's tummy. This is hilarious to baby and big brother, but especially to baby sister. At nine months, any attention is good, but this is the best. She squeals and squeals with rolling laughter, hardly able to catch her breath. The pleasure of making your sister laugh is worth repeating again and again. Big brother laughs, too, and it's a chain reaction as Grandma Donna and I join in the fun.

We will repeat our mistakes of snapping and unsnapping the straps, folding and unfolding the stroller many times, but finally, we get it right, even with some clumsiness and forgetfulness along the way. The kids are not troubled by our misguided attempts. Relax, if they can be patient, so can you. When it comes to your grandchildren, a little fumbling and bumbling is worth it.

IDEAS TO AVOID STRUGGLING
WITH TECHNOLOGY

- *Ask your son or daughter-in-law to make a short how-to video about the car seat, stroller, or any other gizmo that's giving you fits.*

- *Take a computer class or smartphone class at your local community college or online.*

- *Stay connected with family with easy-to-use tech, like Facetime, Skype, WhatsApp, or Zoom.*

- *Call a teenager!*

BOOKS

(Early Learning)

"Once you learn to read, you will be forever free."

FREDERICK DOUGLASS

Every toy store or toy section of any department store has little, thick books with cardboard pages intended for babies. They usually come in square shapes, some in black and white, others in bold, others in contrasting colors, and a few with a little mirror. Some have touchy-feely pages, like a crinkle page or something very soft. My grandchildren probably read all of the best ones long before they could talk, gifted by family, which also included hand-me-downs that were sufficiently classic or precious that they weren't given away.

It's never too early to start reading to the newborn. In a way, I started even before that with my own children. I remember counting, reciting basic addition and subtraction, and even doing multiplication tables when my wife's first pregnancy was advanced, speaking to her tummy. That was until she said, "Enough already!" The firstborn always excelled at math. Who is to say these prenatal recitations weren't a tremendous influence? The secondborn got to listen to all the toddler books read to the firstborn while the secondborn was in the womb. Any wonder why the second child is a true literato devouring a mountain of books? Look at these kids today—one's a doctor and one's a lawyer; and yes, it's a cliché, but isn't that a Jewish mother's dream?

Jews are oft-told, possibly from the pulpit or beginning in Sunday school, that we are the "People of the Book." The "Book" refers to the *Five Books of Moses*, a.k.a. the *Torah*, a.k.a. the *Old Testament*, a.k.a. the *Bible*. Jews may possess a cultural bias about ourselves—that we emphasize education and its corollary; to wit, that we like to read. There may be historical support for this view. As Rabbi Jonathon Sacks wrote, "Throughout the centuries, when the vast majority of Europe was illiterate, Jews maintained an educational infrastructure as their highest priority. It is no exaggeration to say that this lay at the heart of the Jewish ability to survive catastrophe, negotiate change and flourish in difficult circumstances."[3]

Interestingly, however, the phrase, People of the Book, according to Wikipedia, did not originate with Judaism, but with Islam:[4]

> People of the Book or Ahl al-kitāb (Arabic: أهل الكتاب) is an Islamic term referring to followers of those religions which Muslims regard as having been guided by previous revelations, generally in the form of a scripture. In the Quran they are identified as the Jews, the Christians, the Sabians, and—according to some interpretations—the Zoroastrians. Starting from the 8th century, some Muslims also

---

3   Rabbi Jonathon Sacks, *The Dignity of Difference: How to Avoid the Clash of Civilizations*, Bloomsbury Continuum, 2003, p. 139.
4   Wikipedia contributors, "People of the Book," Wikipedia, The Free Encyclopedia, https://en.wikipedia.org/w/index.php?title=People_of_the_Book&oldid=1242449172 (accessed September 22, 2024).

recognized other religious groups such as the Samaritans, and even Buddhists, Hindus, and Jains, as People of the Book.

Thus, it appears that people from all sorts of religious traditions are People of the Book. I intuit that everyone worldwide, given half a chance, values education and likes to read. The love of scholarship is universal among all religions. Presently, according to some researchers, there may be as many as 4,200 organized religions in the world. None of them should fall into the trap of claiming superiority over all of the others when it comes to books. Reading is for everyone.

Pediatric experts overwhelmingly encourage infants and toddlers to read to facilitate language and bonding. Reading to the baby is a fun way to snuggle and a great pastime. It's also a great routine prior to bedtime or naptime, signaling to the little munchkin that it's soon time to conk out.

My grandkids, Eon and Elin, always enjoy a little reading before sleepy time, but they also read books during the day, often several times a day. Before they turned one year old, they seemed to babble and point pretty well at the pictures in their baby books. By that time, they could repeat names and make a lot of animal sounds. They could more or less sing the "ABC Song." By the time they were walking, they could pick which book they wanted to read. What impresses me most is how focused they sometimes seem when I read to them. They definitely get into a zone. I really like the warmth of a little hand on my arm or a little head on my shoulder when we read together.

At age two and three, Eon clearly had favorite books, some that he wanted to read repeatedly, sometimes on the same day. Some of them never got old, at least to him. Others, including the Dr. Seuss books, were pretty long, but still a lot of fun with all the rhymes. Not only did we read the Dr. Seuss books to our kids, but we remembered them from our own childhoods.

Unlike the Dr. Seuss books, some of the books Eon repeatedly chose were...well, kind of boring to the grandparents. We remember one in particular about a train's adventures that went on and on for way too long. We'd roll our eyes at each other each time he picked that book and climbed up on the sofa next to one of us. It just wasn't a very interesting book, but he adored it. When this happens to you, please remember that you are the mature one in the relationship. Demonstrate some patience, for crying out loud. Just read the book. Read it a hundred times if the little guy asks. You are nestled in with a grandchild. The young lad will eventually grow weary of this book (that no adult could possibly enjoy) and move on to another.

I got in the habit, with his most repeated books, of letting Eon finish the sentences every few lines. The animal books also lent themselves to participation with my audience of one, and as Eon got a little older, and my audience doubled with his little sister Elin, they both excelled at making animal sounds, as did I.

Elin is old enough now that she likes to turn the pages. Eon is old enough now that he knows if you accidentally skip a page. He'll grab the suspicious page and turn it back if he thinks it was skipped.

Their dad also introduced them to his *New Yorker* magazine subscription. The weekly magazine has funny cartoons, most captioned, some not, by extremely talented humorists. Once in a while, one of the cartoons really tickles their funny bones. Even if they don't get the cartoon's point, they are primed to laugh if Dad laughs. Sometimes, Dad laughs more when they laugh, and then they laugh even more, proving the adage that laughter is infectious.

As fun as it is to read with Dad or the grandparents, nothing beats reading with Mom. Mom's laughter is intoxicating to her children. Her questions and comments always make it fun for them. You cannot compete with Mom. Grandparents, don't even try.

A time will come when these youngsters grow a little distant, preferring friends or other activities to reading with us. Perhaps all the time spent reading together will become fuzzy memories for them. That will be bittersweet for the grandparents, who will miss a little hand on an arm or a head on a shoulder. But Eon and Elin will always love books, and that is a good thing.

Maybe a day will come when Eon or Elin reads a short story or zine[5] one of them wrote to us. That would tie a giant bow around the gift of family reading and enjoyment.

IDEAS

- *Visit the library or bookstore.*

- *Read out loud to your grandkids at least once every visit, if appropriate.*

- *Play together with letter magnets.*

---

5 A zine is a small self-published work of original or appropriated texts and images usually produced for others who share their interest.

GRANDY'S TOP TEN BOOKS
FOR LITTLE KIDS:

- Goodnight Moon *by Margaret Wise Brown (Author) and Clement Hurd (Illustrator)*

- The Very Hungry Caterpillar *by Eric Carle (Author)*

- Chicka Chicka Boom Boom *by Bill Martin, Jr. (Author), John Archambault (Author), and Lois Ehlert (Illustrator)*

- Where the Wild Things Are *by Maurice Sendak (Author)*

- The Giving Tree *by Shel Silverstein (Author)*

- Are You My Mother? *by P.D. Eastman (Author)*

- Go Dog Go *by P.D. Eastman (Author)*

- The Cat in the Hat *by Dr. Seuss (Author)*

- Yertle the Turtle and Other Stories *by Dr. Seuss (Author)*

- The Lorax *by Dr. Seuss (Author)*

SCREENS

(Fostering Communication)

"Who is rich? He who rejoices in his lot, as it is said:
'You shall enjoy the fruit of your labors, you shall be
happy and you shall prosper.'"
(PSALMS 128:2) ETHICS OF THE FATHERS, 4.1

My early childhood memories of watching television include kid shows with Shari Lewis and Lamb Chop, *Captain Kangaroo*, the *Three Stooges*, and what seemed like an endless parade of Warner Brothers cartoons that ended with, "That's all *folks*!" I also remember adult fare like Giant-Dodger games, presidential nominating conventions, Ed Sullivan, *Bonanza*, Jackie Kennedy's tour of the White House, and the Kennedy, Oswald, and Martin Luther King Jr. assassinations. The TV was on in the afternoon, especially before dinner, and without adult supervision. It was also on every night while my mom knitted and dad read the paper.

Like most households, there was only one TV in our house, planted in the middle of the living room. Five stations were on it consisting of three national networks, one local station, and PBS, which we called by its channel number. I don't remember any restrictions on what or how long we could watch. For example, On Sundays, I watched epic battles between

Wilt Chamberlin and Bill Russell, All-Star Wrestling or Roller Derby, shows of no interest to my parents, who were off doing other things.

The TV screen was black and white and measured thirteen inches. I remember the hoopla when my grandparents bought a color television that was quite a bit bigger, but it suffered from very temperamental reception despite yanking on its antenna this way and that. The coolest feature was a clunky remote control. We had to get up and move the knob to change channels on our TV. My parents held out for a long time on getting a better TV because of the cost.

My children have distinct early memories of what they watched on our twenty-one-inch color TV. We allowed anything on the Disney channel, the two PBS stations, and we had a nice collection of VHS videos of kid movies and kid sing-a-longs acquired over time. We prohibited everything else, especially the commercial cartoon channels, not only because we didn't like some of the dumb programs, but because we really detested the ads. We did not allow video games until the eldest was into his teenage years, which was a point of conflict and whining, and we strictly supervised what was allowed on the early desktop computers. Most importantly, we limited their time watching television to an hour and a half per day.

The result was children who really liked to read, who interacted with other kids and adults pretty well, and greatly excelled in school. The video game prohibition was only mildly effective because they could binge on video games at their friends' homes.

Today, screens are ubiquitous, and my grandchildren's parents are even more restrictive than we were. Their policy for babies and toddlers can be neatly described in two words: NO SCREENS. The no-screens rule applies to televisions, tablets, smartphones, smart watches, video games, laptops and desktops. No screens literally means no screens when the kids are around.

I initially ran smack dab afoul of this policy during a visit to see the newborn, when our son and his wife lived in a different state. I brought my tablet on the trip to follow my favorite sports team. I had a subscription to stream their games. My son said I couldn't hold the baby if I was watching the game on my iPad. He also caught Grandma looking at her smartphone in proximity to the baby, and she received the same stern correction.

As new grandparents, we instinctually wanted to abide by the new parents' rules. Later, we learned that many, if not most, contemporary parents are aware of neurological findings or independently intuit that screen time is detrimental to developing language skills, attention span, and creativity. This does not seem surprising. I don't know when I first heard the expression "boob tube," but the term became part of the common lexicon years ago. A boob was slang for an idiot, and someone watching a lot of TV was clearly wasting a lot of time with the boob tube. Television was somewhat akin to a baby sucking a pacifier. Accordingly, limiting the amount of time kids watched television was a thing long before our grandchildren were born. Why shouldn't the contemporary parent apply the same concept to the variety and proliferation of screens?

In 2019, the World Health Organization (WHO) published guidelines recommending that children under two should not be exposed to *any* electronic screens, and that children ages two to four should have no more than one hour of sedentary screen time per day—the less, the better.[6] If you look it up, which, knowing my son and his wife, they probably did,

6   Emily S. Rueb, "W.H.O. Says Limited or No Screen Time for Children Under 5," *The New York Times,* April 24, 2019 https://www.nytimes.com/2019/04/24/health/screen-time-kids.html.

screen time for infants leads to a parade of "horribles," all impacting physical, emotional, and cognitive development.

Interestingly, my son and his wife also started limiting their own screen time after the birth of their first child. They drastically reduced their cable TV bill. Whether this occurred due to a new-found frugality or just occurred organically because of the age of streaming, I cannot say. Their newborn little miracle dominated their time away from work. Clearly, when parents fall in love with their newborn children, they may prefer providing the baby their full attention rather than dividing it with a television, laptop, or smartphone.

Video calls are exceptions to the no-screen-time rule. That's great as long as the phone or tablet doesn't freeze mid-call. (I wonder what a baby or toddler thinks when the technology goes haywire.) Video calls with a person of limited vocabulary might not last very long, but grandparents can still connect with enthusiastic hellos, smiles, laughter, and waves. My favorite wave is when I bend my index finger up and down. My grandchildren recognize it as a special wave and an easy wave to return. The finger wave always seems to evoke a smile or at least a response.

Speaking of smiles, when a grandchild smiles at his or her grandparent, even if it's during a video call, any feeling of loneliness or isolation dissipates from the person's consciousness, like the clouds parting on a gray day. And when the little person's smile is accompanied by a giggle or a laugh, it's like the sun coming out and taking away the chill. You can feel the warmth even if you're only looking at a screen.

My grandson's favorite question on a video call, if only one grand-parent is visible on his end, is, "Where's Gwandma Donna?" or "Where's Grandy?" He insists on seeing both grandparents. He might also ask to see the family dogs.

During my grandkids' tender years, I learned that yes or no questions were a lot easier for our grandchildren to handle than open-ended ones. A two-year-old can answer, "Did you just take a bath?" a lot easier than, "What did you do today?" Also, when the toddler turns his or her head away from you, it may express a feeling of being overwhelmed, just like when that happens in person.

Elin, at age one plus, seems very interested in staring at us on a video call. We might or might not get much of a finger wave, but with a parent's urging, we can get a hello and goodbye hand wave. She's not yet ready to make funny faces with Grandma Donna, but that doesn't stop Grandma from trying.

Approaching age three, Eon is quick to announce that, "I am not a boy, grwwww!" "He's a bear," clarifies Mom, off-screen. "I'm a lion, grwwww!" I then respond. "I'm a wolf," says Grandma Donna, "Ahwooo!" The growling and howling are the gist of that conversation.

Another time, both kids were standing on their toddler step stool in the kitchen. This is a special step stool with rails and an anti-slip mat so the kids can see what's happening on the kitchen counters. The kids were busy snacking on mandarin oranges as Dad made dinner. They were hungry, and the orange pieces were delicious. They didn't have much to say during this video call.

One bonus of video calls is you never know what the people you're calling will be doing or where they are. You get a candid look at a day in the life of grandchildren, parents or grandparents.

When the call comes to an end, Eon always likes to be the one to touch the exit button ending the call.

IDEAS

- *Discuss the right amount of video call time with your grandkids' parents so everyone is on the same page.*

- *Talk to your grandkids about screen time—ask them what they like about it and what they don't like about it. Educate them about the benefits and drawbacks of using it.*

FURTHER READING

See, from the National Library of Medicine, "Effects of Excessive Screen Time on Child Development: An Updated Review and Strategies for Management." https://www.ncbi.nlm.nih.gov/pmc/articles/PMC10353947/

See, from the Mayo Clinic, "Screen Time and Children: How to Guide Your Child." https://www.mayoclinic.org/healthy-lifestyle/childrens-health/in-depth/screen-time/art-20047952

EX-KA-VAY-DOR!

(Vocabulary)

A grandparent might say to a grandchild,
"A leben ahf dein kepele!"
(Literally, a life on your head! Meaning, you are so smart!)

I really try not to brag about how smart my grandchildren are. I might tell you something they said, but I think I'll keep how phenomenally intelligent they are to myself. (Whoops, sorry, I guess I let the cat out of the bag.) Psychologists might say that bragging stems from a need for validation and approval. I don't need to brag about these grandkids because just being around them is validation enough. However, when it comes to kvelling, going on and on about the grandkids, I'm like anyone else. A grandparent doesn't require anyone's pre-approval, just like you can't seal off a natural spring from the water bubbling up.

I also love to see our grandchildren's interplay with their parents, which is repeated numerous times a day. One classic example is every time the parents come home after work. Parents, babies, and toddlers can't help but light up for each other. It's automatic.

As grandparents, we also always feel flattered and thrilled when our grandchildren are excited to see us. Eon, our two-and-one-half-year-old, knows when we are coming. He stands on the sofa by the living room's picture window, jumping up and down as we walk up to the house. Elin, his little sister, isn't even one year old, but she smiles whenever she sees someone she knows. Her smiles are special—what a sweetheart!

Of course, with Eon, you have to listen very carefully, as his vocabulary has outpaced his articulation. He likes to point out what is happening on the street as you walk a couple of blocks to get takeout. He might point out a mail truck or a guy on a bicycle. He will surely look up and let you know about a helicopter or an airplane. He is able to spot construction cranes off in the distance. His pronunciation may not be perfect, but if you are listening, he is spot-on with his observations.

At a birthday party for Eon's older cousin, my daughter-in-law's mom, Grandma Dianne, was dishing out the ice cream to accompany the slices of birthday cake. Everyone was picking between chocolate cookie dough and vanilla mint chocolate chip. "Eon, do you want the chocolate or the vanilla, the brown one or the white one?" she asked. Eon, who had been patiently waiting for the cake and ice cream ever since he arrived at the party, suddenly hesitated, at odds with his normal lightning-quick reactions. You could see the wheels turning. Finally, he raised and held out both index fingers on each hand. "One and one," he told his grandmother. Of course, he wanted both—why pick just one?

Perhaps creative vocabulary runs in the family. Years and years ago, my son was three, and my wife was pregnant. My pickup truck could not seat four of us with two car seats. It had to go. I explained to him that we were trading in the pickup for an SUV. He wanted to understand what the new car was going to look like. I tried explaining what the SUV was, using the pickup as a baseline, explaining the extra seats instead of a pickup bed. After a little description, he grasped the idea. "A squished-in truck!" he exclaimed.

On another occasion, my younger son, approaching age three, overheard visitors at the zoo wonder aloud about an animal that they called a cross between a monkey and a raccoon. He couldn't help but chime in. "That's a ring-tailed lemur," he said matter-of-factly.

Eon, age two plus, also surprises with his powers of observation and vocabulary. On a walk to the local takeout place with me, a flatbed truck carrying heavy construction equipment stopped at a red light. "Ex-ka-vay-dor!" yelled Eon over the traffic noise. Indeed, it wasn't a loader or a backhoe; it was, in fact, an excavator.

Like his Ti-Ti, his dad's brother, who knew the names of all the animals, Eon was an early and astounding book learner. He especially loved our laminated *Mac's Field Guide* with pictures of all the good and bad garden bugs. He was quick to call out the names of the bad bugs he might see outdoors, like the potato beetle, earwig, green aphid, or green stink bug, all bad bugs, according to *Mac's*. He likewise got excited seeing *Mac's* good garden bugs like the dragonfly, ladybug, yellow jacket, or centipede.

Eon also was always on the lookout for spider webs. He liked how delicately patterned and shiny they were, but deduced spiders might be nearby, a prospect he found distressing. He was definitely scared of spiders. Yet, when we turned over rocks on a salt-water beach to look for little crabs when the tide was out, he loved picking them up without a hint of trepidation. He liked to carry and release them down at the water's edge. "They're like ocean spiders," he said, clearly not experiencing any concerns.

Eon didn't like going to bed. In a nutshell, Mom and Dad were too much fun. Sometimes, Dad made a bargain. They could do a science experiment if Eon would brush his teeth, go to the bathroom, and hit the hay after just one book. Dad set out a glass, cooking oil, and water on the table. Mom found some food coloring she had used when she made cookies. Dad let Eon pour water into the glass, then cooking oil, stir, and then use a dropper for just a few drops of the food coloring. They went step by step, asking Eon to guess what might happen before each step and to say what happened after. He was surprised when the oil and the colored water separated. Once the experiment was all done, Eon exclaimed, "That's science!" trotting off to his bedroom, as his parents beamed with pride.

IDEAS

- *Avoid baby talk: use full phrases and sentences, e.g., "Da-Da go?" "Yes, Daddy is putting on his shoes and going to work now."*

- *Read menus and street signs together. When taking items out of a grocery bag, ask grandkids to name each one, and describe what they see and what they feel when they touch the item. Ask them how the item is used.*

- *Listen closely—look at your toddler when they speak and respond to what they say.*

- *Read more books!*

MEAN TRACTOR

(Patience and Aggressive Play)

"On ne saurait faire d'omelette sans casser des œufs."

("You can't make an omelette without breaking eggs.")

FRANÇOIS DE CHARETTE

One variation of playing cars with Eon was called Mean Tractor. Mean Tractor was a matchbox-sized tractor resembling a John Deere mower. Mean Tractor didn't like to play with any of the other matchbox cars. Instead, Mean Tractor liked to bang into the other cars hard enough that they fell on the floor and had to go to the hospital. "I'm Mean Tractor," roared Eon in his falsetto, growly voice, which was sometimes a bear and sometimes a lion, as he smashed Mean Tractor into another car.

An ambulance and police car were parked with each other on a nearby pillow. As cars suffered Mean Tractor's attacks, they often got an owie, Eon's preferred term for an injury. Once assaulted, it was my job or Grandma Donna's to voice a pathetic, "Wah!" the injured car's cry. After they got an owie, "Wee-woo, wee-woo," came the police car right away. Then, "Wee-woo, wee-woo," came the ambulance right behind. Eon magically transported the injured vehicle through the air to the hospital, a ringed area on the floor made with blocks. There, Eon asked me or Grandma Donna where the owie was, e.g., on the door, the hood, the trunk, or the engine. The ambulance had to touch the owie with the correctly colored, imaginary band-aid:

Eon: What color band-aid do you want, Grandy?

Grandy: A green one.

"Okay..."

Eon carefully opened and closed the back door of the ambulance before the imaginary band-aid was applied, with the ambulance car gently touching the owie on the injured car.

"...Sssss," said Eon, which magically healed the injury.

But what if the ambulance didn't have the requested color of band-aid?

Eon: I have yellow and red, but no green ones.

Grandy: No, I only want a green one, please.

Eon: I'll have to go to the store!

Grandy: Well, when you're there, do you mind getting some things for dinner?

Eon: Yes, I'll get kale, beets, and cilantro for dinner."

This child clearly had some adult tastes.

Grandy: Should we play cooking now?

Cooking is another one of Eon's favorite fantasy games.

Eon: No, we're playing Mean Tractor!

How silly to suggest changing the game to cooking! How could one possibly get bored playing Mean Tractor?

The truth was Grandma Donna and I never felt completely comfortable playing Mean Tractor. The unease came from a feeling of shock and surprise that our little sweet pea, our *mensch* of a grandson, could delight in a mean and aggressive game. Still, the game also involved compassion. Mean Tractor inflicted injuries, but the emergency vehicles were there to get the injured party to the hospital and patch things up with multi-colored band-aids.

The question also arises: How long can a three-year-old explore the same scenario with Mean Tractor hitting the other nice cars, followed by the wee-woo sirens of the police and ambulance, and band-aids of different colors? We felt bored playing the same game over and over, especially when it made us a little uncomfortable. Eon's Uncle Ti-Ti, for example, refused to play Mean Tractor. He told Eon to play something else, because hitting toys wasn't nice, a lesson that would come in handy when he played with other boys and girls.

We reasoned a little differently. Yes, the kid was playing aggressively, but he wasn't hurting himself or anybody else. They were his toys. He wasn't breaking them, but if one broke, wouldn't that be a good lesson? We thought it better to bite our tongues. Perhaps this is an example of the admonition in Ecclesiastes (7:8-9): "…better to have a patient spirit than a haughty one. Don't let your spirit be quickly vexed, for vexation resides in the hearts of fools."

After all, isn't the very definition of patience the ability to hang in there when uncomfortable? We also rationalized that we didn't want to discourage this imaginative three-year-old from wanting to play with us in the future. We saw that this little kid was practicing his motor skills, vocabulary, creativity, memory, aggressiveness, and empathy, all rolled into one game. Aggressiveness and empathy are part and parcel of the human condition, almost two sides of the same coin. Isn't that worth a little patience?

As grandparents, we'd love it if our little *mensch* acted lovingly 24/7, but that isn't realistic. As young as he is, he knows not to throw things. Those instances garner an immediate response. Mom and Dad have amply explained how throwing things might hurt someone and is simply not allowed, using their very serious faces and voices. He also knows he isn't supposed to push or shove his peers. The general rule is not to do anything that might hurt someone. When his baby sister was born, he was told over and over to be gentle. In a heart-melting way, he liked to softly hug his little sister.

The American Academy of Pediatrics informs us that aggressive behavior, including some emotional outbursts, is normal for toddlers.[7] Aggressive behavior, according to the experts, is often a way of testing social skills and expressing fears, emotions, or frustrations. Aggressive behavior may be the child's attempt at control and independence.

Even though our uneasiness caused us to try to steer Eon from playing Mean Tractor, Eon ignored these suggestions. He determinedly wanted to play Mean Tractor. Repeatedly, we patiently played along.

Still, we wondered why Mean Tractor was so mean. Finally, Grandma Donna asked:

Grandma Donna: Is Mean Tractor so mean because he doesn't have any friends?

Eon: No.

7   Resources for Advancing Mental Health in Pediatrics, "Understanding and Treating Aggression in Children," https://ramp.luriechildrens.org/en/conditions-and-treatments/diagnoses-and-conditions/understanding-aggression-in-children/ (accessed September 22, 2024).
   Cleveland Clinic, "Have an Aggressive Toddler? Here's How To Manage Their Behavior," June 25, 2024, https://health.clevelandclinic.org/toddler-hitting-and-aggressive-behavior.

Grandma Donna: Is Mean Tractor mean because he's hungry?

Eon: No.

Grandma Donna: Is Mean Tractor so mean because he's tired?

Eon: No.

Grandma Donna: Is Mean Tractor always going to be mean?

Eon: No.

Grandma Donna: Well, why is Mean Tractor so mean?

Eon: Mean Tractor drank too much coffee.

Grandma Donna: Oh, Mean Tractor drank too much coffee?

Eon: Yeah.

Grandma Donna: Ah-ha, thank you for clarifying! Now we know. Good to know.

Eon's aggressive play did not mean that we were falling short of raising a good human being. In fact, he was teaching us—we coffee-addicted Seattleites—that maybe we should drink a little more decaf.

IDEAS

- *Identify and validate difficult feelings: "I see that you are feeling frustrated."*

- *Avoid getting triggered yourself—stay calm and ask what is bothering them.*

- *Set limits about what is ok behavior and what is not. Be firm and discuss with parents if need be.*

FURTHER READING

See, "When To Worry About Toddler Aggression" by Emily Fromm, reviewed by Wayne Fleisig, Ph.D. See, https://www.parents.com/toddlers-preschoolers/discipline/improper-behavior/taming-toddler-aggression/

BASKET HEAD

(Laughter)

"Time spent playing with a child is never wasted."

ANONYMOUS

A laundry basket is often used in a growing family. Laundry is an ongoing and seemingly never-ending chore. When we were babysitting for a full day at our kids' place, we liked to help with the laundry. We found that Eon, at age two-and-one-half, was already familiar with the process of folding, sorting, and putting away. He was happy to be our little helper. He knew whose clothes belonged to him, Elin, Mom, or Dad and where to put them away. We never considered doing some laundry with Eon as much of a learning moment, but as just another extension of playing and hanging out together.

In fact, here's a list of life skills from a Montessori website that describes what little ones learn from folding clothes:[8]

---

8 The Global Montessori Network, "Folding and Putting Away Clothes," https:// theglobalmontessorinetwork.org/resource/parents/putting-away-clothes-english/ (accessed September 22, 2024).

1. It teaches them to be neat and organized. They will be able to put their clothes away in their drawers and closets neatly instead of just throwing them on the floor or on top of the dresser.
2. It teaches them that they need to take care of their belongings.
3. It teaches them responsibility because they need to make sure that they put the clothes away when they are done with them so that other people can use them later on.
4. It teaches them patience because folding takes time, and patience is a good quality for everyone.
5. It teaches them the value of hard work because they put in the effort to do a good job and make their clothes neat.

According to the website, that's not all; they are also:

-   Learning unfamiliar words and improving language skills
-   Taking and following directions
-   Counting and sequencing
-   Identifying similarities and differences
-   Sorting like items into groups
-   Identifying shapes (and forming new ones)
-   Taking charge and doing daily household chores

Wow—and we thought we were just folding the laundry! Thank you, Montessori folks, for thinking through child development so thoroughly. I would take exception, however, to the idea that doing some laundry was "hard work." It did not seem very challenging to Eon. It seemed almost as mundane a chore to him as to us. It also didn't take very long to fill and empty a basket of clothes.

Leave it to Eon to decide what to do next. He took the laundry basket, flipped it onto his head, and said, "I'm Basket Head!"

The laundry basket was a normal-sized rectangle, and although it had a lot of ventilation holes in it, undoubtedly to make it lighter, lifting and placing a laundry basket on your head with the muscles of a two-and-one-half-year-old took some effort.

That Eon transformed himself into Basket Head so quickly was exceedingly funny to him. Basket Head was sashaying around the room, looking through the holes of the laundry basket and saying, "Hmmm," between giggles.

Although his laugh was infectious, the adults in the room were conflicted. This was happening on our watch. Witnessing our precious grandchild waltzing around as Basket Head created an internal alarm bell for a risk of injury. On the other hand, he was laughing so much that he fell down, with the laundry basket spilling onto the floor without any damage to the child or anything else.

How could we refrain from laughing and spoil the fun? Seeing our smiles, and true to the nature of a two-and-one-half-year-old, Eon became Basket Head again and again. He put the laundry basket on his head and took a few steps, laughing. Eventually, he spoke in his falsetto voice of a make-believe growling lion, "I'm Basket Head!" Then he'd fall over. His funniest moment came when he ran into the wall, because he was laughing so much and didn't see where he was going. This, too, was as unexpected as Eon becoming Basket Head in the first place and brought forth still more laughter.

I doubt the Basket Head game will be listed on a Montessori website anytime soon, but if it were, the bullet points for Basket Head might be:

- Learning how to make yourself and your grandparents laugh
- Creating a new game
- Building arm strength and balance
- Practicing falling down without getting hurt
- Experiencing the folly of running into things
- Exploring the absurdity of life

In subsequent visits, Eon didn't play Basket Head. I wonder if his parents put a quick end to this game or if putting the laundry basket on his head was simply a one-off.

Eon, however, invented plenty of other games. One game involved stacking books and toys on me when I sat on the sofa in the living room. Eon ran out of the living room, through the dining room, turned left at the kitchen, and dashed into the playroom. Why walk when you can run? There, he picked up as many favorite cars or dinosaur figurines as he could to bring into the living room for me to hold. Soon, I couldn't hold any more. I was buried with books and toys that were hard to keep balanced and from falling off onto the floor. Eon decided it was as much fun to run the items back to the playroom once there wasn't anywhere else on me to put anything.

Another game was when Eon had to go to work. He put "baby," a stuffed animal he always slept with, down his shirt and pulled his wagon in a circle around the dining room and the hall and back into the living room. "I'm going to work!" he shouted, pulling his wagon in circles. Eon loved running back and forth, pulling his wagon, over and over again. All that was required of Grandma Donna or me was to say, "Have a good day at work, see you later!"

Basket Head made a reappearance a couple of months later in the playroom. This time, Eon used a wicker basket, smaller than a laundry basket, about three-quarters as tall as he was, that was used to store toys. It had little side handles. Unlike the laundry basket, he couldn't see through the wicker basket, but it balanced on his shoulders when he put it on his head and held the handles, so he could look down and see the floor. Again, he roared like a lion, "I am Basket Head!" as he exited the playroom and went through the kitchen to reenter the playroom from the hallway, a circular route. The clear highlight of this game was running around and back to Grandma Donna and me in the playroom, where he dramatically fell into our laps as the basket fell off. Eon invited brief hugs and tummy tickles before getting up and doing it again and again.

By the time Eon reaches elementary school, I doubt that he'll remember playing Basket Head. I probably wouldn't remember either, if not for this memoir. Eon will graduate to other creative and fulfilling play, but I hope that he never loses his inner joy, his infectious laugh, his charisma, and spontaneity. I don't think he will. It appears ingrained in his personality. He knows how to laugh and to lift the spirits of those he's with.

IDEAS

- *See, Set the Stage for a Lifetime of Laughter.*

    https://www.stlouischildrens.org/health-resources/pulse/set-stage-lifetime-laughter

- *See, Encouraging Your Child's Sense of Humor.*

    https://www.childrensmn.org/educationmaterials/parents/article/10289/encouraging-your-childs-sense-of-humor/

- *Create a story with your kid(s), and then have them dress up as one of the characters and act it out.*

- *Do something surprising and silly, e.g., put a shoe on your hand and a hat on your foot.*

JOKIC

(Sports)

"A point makes you happy; an assist makes you and your teammate happy. An assist makes two people happy."

NIKOLA JOKIC

We were missing the grandkids. We'd met up at a park at a half-way place between where we all lived. We walked around with Eon, aged two-and-a-half, as we pushed Elin, aged eight months, in the stroller through the park. After his dad told him about bamboo, Eon wanted to know the names of many of the plants. Dad's smartphone identified most of the different plants that we couldn't name. By the time we'd gone up and down and around the trail, it was lunchtime.

We found a grille a few miles away with a kid's menu. The kids' menu had chicken strips with fries and a fruit cup. Elin liked dipping her food into the ranch dressing. The restaurant wasn't really a sports bar, but it had a few mounted televisions showing a basketball game. "Jokic!" exclaimed Eon, pointing to basketball players on the TV.

Eon and his parents lived in Denver for a number of years while his parents earned their advanced degrees. Eon's parents became big Denver Nuggets fans and especially enjoyed the team's center, Nikola Jokic, a

280-pound, lumbering seven-footer with a feathery touch around the basket. He wasn't fast, and he didn't jump very high. He lacked even the average athleticism for most NBA players, but he could pass to open teammates like he had eyes in the back of his head, which was very special for any player, but especially for a guy that big. He genuinely liked passing more than scoring.

"Yes, that's a basketball game on the TV, but Jokic isn't playing in that game. That's another game," explained Eon's dad.

Eon and Elin's screen time was severely limited by their parents. But there was one exception. Sometimes, as a special treat, Eon got to watch a few minutes of a Nuggets game before bedtime. Elin was usually already in bed.

"Do you want to watch a little basketball before bed, Eon?" asked his parents.

"I want to watch so, so much," pleaded Eon with his happy and charming smile.

"Okay, let's watch five minutes before bed."

"Ten!" said Eon.

"Okay, ten," said Dad, "but then right to bed, okay?"

"Okay."

How do you say no to a two-and-a-half-year-old who knows his numbers well enough to bargain for more time?

Eon snuggled on the couch with his parents watching the game, asking the names of other players or why a play was called a foul. He didn't like going to bed, but he didn't put up much of a fuss when he got to do something special, like watching Jokic or doing a science experiment, before bedtime.

Eon's dad grew up with parents who passionately watched the

basketball playoffs. When Eon's dad was only around two-and-a-half years old, in 1991, Michael Jordan and the Bulls ended the Laker's championship runs with Magic Johnson. He doesn't remember, but his parents vividly recall that he called Magic Johnson, "Mayi-ah-hoo." When Eon's dad was only seven years old, wearing his Shawn Kemp Sonics jersey, he got to see Michael Jordan in the finals at Key Arena, a remodeled old stadium in Seattle Center. He vividly recalls how loud it was.

I have seen a lot of games over the years. I remember dragging my parents, Eon's great grandparents, to San Francisco's Civic Auditorium when Rick Barry starred alongside Nate Thurmond and Al Attles for the San Francisco Warriors. Basketball fandom has been passed down through three generations.

In 2006, the billionaire owner of the Sonics (and biggest stockholder of the Starbucks corporation) misguidedly sold the Sonics to oilmen from Oklahoma, simultaneously selling us fans down the river. But he paved the way for us to fully enjoy stars on other teams, like Steph Curry and Lebron James. Steph and Lebron's best teams performed a kind of ballet, an artistry of the collective, with teammates all in sync. As their stars began to fade, and because part of my family lived in Denver, it was natural to gravitate to Jokic because of his team-first, unique, and talented passing style.

Given this history, I couldn't wait until Eon was old enough to gift him a little tykes basketball hoop. It came with three soft, six-inch rubber balls. The stand was three feet high and blue with an oversized orange rim. You had to fill the base with sand so it wouldn't tip over. If Eon stood on his tippy toes, he could just dunk the ball.

Unbeknownst to me, Eon's dad bought Eon a very similar basketball set the very same month, not proving that great minds think alike, but that the game, at least in this family, is in the blood. We quickly decided it was nice for Eon to have a basketball hoop at each house, at Mom and Dad's outside on the patio, and at ours inside in the family room.

Visits at either place often included some hoop time. Every time Eon made a basket, he said, "Two points!" or "Dunk," while his grandfather and father said things like, "Nothing but net! Swish," or "Three pointer." Eon was very good at running to retrieve any shot that bounced away and throwing it back to his older playmates.

Seattle is a great basketball city despite the Sonics fans being sold down the river by a greedy owner. Sue Bird, a five-time Olympic Gold Medal winner, who happens to also be Jewish and has dual citizenship with Israel, has consistently been beloved in Seattle during the Sonics' absence. She starred and played her entire career for the Seattle Storm, winning three titles in three different decades. She epitomized unselfish play and how a point guard can keep her team motivated and connected.

Eon and his little sister Elin come from a family of average height. We don't know what team sports, if any, they may play in the future, but chances are pretty slim that they will play competitive basketball at a college or professional level. It doesn't matter. Right now, they love running around, whether outside or inside. They have such a great time at the neighborhood playground that I think they are going to like some sort of athletics when they get older.

Are they likely to develop a love of organized sports? When they get much older, will they be imbued with the worthiness of team play? Will they spot a teammate who is open? They already seem to enjoy an innate sense of fairness, and they like following directions. Eon will like it when Elin gets a little older to facilitate their play together; perhaps they will be like Reggie and Cheryl Miller when they play little tykes basketball. As young as they are, they play pretty well with each other most of the time, despite the usual sibling rivalry in regard to grabbing toys.

Their mom and her siblings are long-distance runners, including an uncle who ran the Boston Marathon. Mom's running has inspired their dad and his brother, Ti-Ti, to also go for frequent runs, though neither can keep up with Eon and Elin's Mom. She's fast and fit. To date, so are her kids. They are likely to remain fast and fit as they grow into adulthood. The question is, if they grow to play team sports, will they pass the ball?

IDEAS

- *Consider coaching a team that your grandkids would like to be on.*

- *Talk to your grandkids' school at the beginning of each school year to see what opportunities might exist for getting them involved in team sports, dance or individual sports like gymnastics.*

- *Be on the outlook for what kind of activities your grandkids gravitate to naturally, and support and encourage those.*

- *See if the parents want to sign up your grandkids for swimming lessons—volunteer to take them.*

- *For toddlers, stand in a circle and practice passing the ball.*

FURTHER READING

See, "How to Easily Stop Selfishness in Basketball." *See*, https://www.basketballforcoaches.com/selfish-basketball/

DOGS AND BABES

(Furry Friends)

"Happiness is a warm puppy."

CHARLES M. SCHULZ

Are dogs compatible with infants and toddlers? It goes without saying that you'd never leave a baby on the floor in a room with a dog or in any area, unattended, with any dog, no matter how mellow the pet. Dogs have been called man's best friend due to the unique relationship developed between humans and dogs over thousands of years, but how well do they get along with babies? In many cultures, dogs get a bad rap, and not in relation to little humans.

In Jewish literature, dogs were condemned for snarling and prowling about at night (Psalms 59:7), for gluttony (Isaiah 56:11), for laziness and stupidity (Isaiah 56:10), and for a lack of hygiene (Proverbs 26:11). Calling a person a dog was definitely an insult: "As dogs return to their own vomit, so fools repeat their folly." (Proverbs 26:11) A favorite Jewish proverb states, "Lie down with dogs, get up with fleas."

Perhaps these dramatic and consistently negative portrayals of dogs help explain my personal observations of highly orthodox Jews who lack experience with dogs and appear genuinely afraid, even when the friendliest of dogs might come up sniffing just to say hello. Not so for those of us in the diaspora who grew up with a family dog and have enjoyed dogs for many decades in our families. In my experience as a child and adult, each dog was so integrated into our family that I could write a chapter about each one.

My all-time favorite of all our family dogs is Splash, a Nova Scotia Duck Tolling Retriever. Tollers are like golden retrievers—only a little smaller and a little smarter. Splash is an auburn-reddish-orange-brown color that spectacularly glistens in the sun. She also has beautiful eyes, runs like the wind, and nestles in between my legs on an ottoman when I'm reading. One adult child calls her chorizo (sausage), claiming she's a tad overweight, to needle his father about what I admit might be viewed as an excessive affection for this dog. This description, however, contrasts with those of absolute strangers who spontaneously comment on the dog's beauty and her lovely eyes.

I love Splash in almost all respects, but she has one annoying quality. She becomes hysterical when family comes to visit or when she spies a rabbit. The Toller scream, as it's called, is a shrill, ear-piercing cry, as opposed to a normal dog's bark, and it's as loud as a fire alarm. She has never caught a rabbit, but that does not deter her hysterical excitement when she sees one through the window. Her running mate, my wife's dog, Nova, a loving but hypertense Portuguese Water Dog, has a hair-trigger bark anytime she is excited. Her bark is also irritatingly high-pitched, an offending, loud yip, so when they both spy a rabbit outside from inside the house, the joint frenzy is deafening. You just have to open the door to let them fly out and run it off.

When my son and his family arrive at our house, little ones in tow, Splash goes berserk with her Toller scream, and Nova joins in with her unfortunate barking or vice-versa. Which of the two starts the mad cacophony is anyone's guess, because the other joins in instantly. Together, they provide a horrible greeting to our beloved son, daughter-in-law, and grandchildren. Accordingly, their parents hold both of the kids in their arms until the dogs run around outside enough to settle down. Otherwise, the obvious risk is that one of the dogs might knock over a precious grandchild.

Kudos to our grandchildren, Eon and Elin, as they navigate their way to the family room and the two baskets of toys, while the adults in the room are commanding, "Nova, knock it off!" or, "Splash, go lie down!" At this point in the visit, the babes are a curiosity with such great smells that the dogs continue to overdo their greetings, communicated by a lot of sniffing. Eon and Elin are familiar with pets because of their family's cat, Turkey, who was taken in as a stray, bedraggled kitten, and their family's dog, Jelly, a loving and goofy Berna doodle. Both took up residence with their parents before the grandchildren were born.

Turkey and Jelly have always been entirely respectful when a new baby invaded their home turf. They intuited the baby's helplessness and preciousness, and observed their masters' love, awe, and devotion to the new member of the family.

Similarly, Splash and Nova know where our kids and grandkids stand in the hierarchy of sentient beings comprising our family. Indeed, this may explain the heightened excitement of the dogs when the family comes to visit. Again, as sweet and easygoing as these dogs and any other dogs may be in their usual calm state, we would never leave them alone with the grandkids.

Splash and Nova have learned to hover around kitchen counters during mealtime preparation and the kitchen table during mealtimes in the sometimes-realized hope that a morsel of food may drop on the floor upon which they can pounce. Grandchildren are a bonanza in their highchairs, certain to drop a little or a lot of food that didn't quite make it into their mouths or fall into the pocket of the bib as they utilize their baby spoons and forks.

I love it when Elin spontaneously says, "Splash" or "Nova." It makes me think she likes them or at least includes them in her world. One of her brother's very first and oft-repeated words was "Jelly." The kids clearly see Jelly as another member of their family; as such, they likewise accept their grandparents' dogs. They have grown up with parents frequently walking the dog while they enjoy the view of the neighborhood from the stroller.

Eon is old enough now that he likes to throw the ball for Splash or watch me use the chuck-it. Splash brings the ball back every time. Playing fetch makes Splash happy, letting her run fast and satisfying her retrieval instinct. Eon likes making Splash chase and delights in her doing what *he* wants her to. Splash doesn't just drop the ball, but she isn't comfortable yet handing the ball to Eon. She hands it to me, and I give it to Eon to throw.

The psychological benefits for humans living with pets like dogs and cats are well-studied and beyond argument. But what about pets and little kids? A frequently cited study from Australia in *Pediatric Research* found that children with dogs were roughly 30 percent less likely to have conduct problems, 40 percent less likely to have difficulty relating to peers, and 34 percent more likely to show positive social behaviors.[9]

9 Hayley Christian, PhD, et al., "Pets Are Associated with Fewer Peer Problems and Emotional Symptoms, and Better Prosocial Behavior: Findings from the Longitudinal Study of Australian Children," *The Journal of Pediatrics*, May 2020, https://www.jpeds.com/article/S0022-3476(20)30025-1/fulltext.

Interestingly, studies also show that babies catch fewer colds, get fewer ear infections, and need fewer antibiotics in their first year of life in homes with dogs. Other research shows that living with dogs as an infant may lower the risk of developing allergies and asthma.[10] Perhaps dogs and cats often provide just the right amount of exposure to germs and allergens early on, fortifying the immune systems of little people.

Insulting people by comparing them to animals like snakes, leeches, and rats is an unfortunate part of our lexicon. And with all due respect to the above-cited biblical and Talmudic references about canines, let's stop describing people as subhuman by comparing them to dogs. Infants and toddlers, devoid of prejudices, know the family dog is an important member of the family.

The great Jewish sages valued all members of the animal kingdom.[11] Maimonides, also known as the Rambam, was an affluent Sephardic rabbi, physician, and philosopher who became one of the most influential Torah scholars of the Middle Ages. Maimonides wrote:

"There is no difference between the pain of humans and the pain of other living beings, since the love and tenderness of the mother for the young are not produced by reasoning, but by feeling."

The Baal Shem Tov was a venerated Jewish mystic who is regarded as the founder of Chasidic Judaism. The Baal Shem Tov said:

10 Susanna Block, "Pets are good for kids; here's why | Ask the Pediatrician," *Seattle's Child*, Updated April 25, 2024, https://www.seattleschild.com/pets-are-good-for-kids-heres-why-ask-the-pediatrician/.
11 In fact, in Judaism the Sabbath commandment to rest on the seventh day also applies to working animals—ox, ass, and cattle.

"A man should consider himself as a worm, and all other small animals his friends in the world, for all them are all created."

These wise and holy righteous men of yesteryear know what my grandchildren have grown up knowing. Canine, feline, and human alike, we are all a part of a living, breathing world of sentient beings. We all have feelings, nobody's perfect, and we should all be friends, members of the same family.

DOG TIPS WORTH TEACHING

- *Show how to approach the family dog and pet gently.*

- *Leave the dog alone when it is eating.*

- *Never touch a dog through a fence.*

- *Don't run up to a dog.*

- *Keep your face away from a dog.*

- *If a dog is chasing you, stop running.*

- *Let kids help you take care of your dog—show them how to brush and feed your pup!*

- ***Never leave a baby, infant, or toddler unattended with a dog.***

AARDVARK

(Grandparent Anxiety)

"If there is anxiety in a person's heart, let him quash it."
(PROVERBS 12:25)

*"Rabbi Ami and Rabbi Asi dispute the verse's meaning. One said:
He should forcefully push it [the anxiety] out of his mind. One who
worries should banish his concerns from his thoughts. And [the other]
one said: It means he should tell others his concerns,
which will lower his anxiety."*
TALMUD, YOMA 75A:2

I rarely suffer any moderate to severe anxiety during my waking hours.
I process that level of anxiety in dreams. Most of the time, I can't remember
what was happening in the dream after a matter of seconds or within a
minute of waking up, but in that little window, I feel my quickened pulse
and a kind of disorienting dread, simultaneously recalling the thinnest
thread of the dream.

Thus, I dreamed that I lost Aardvark. Do not confuse the Aardvark
in my dream with the actual animal that's hard to picture that lives God
knows where, called the aardvark. The Aardvark I lost was a little person,

a precious being, a grandson around age five, and then alternately, my granddaughter around age three. I don't know how they changed from one to the other in the dream, but they did. In real life, my grandson was only age one-and-a-half, and my granddaughter hadn't quite been born yet. My daughter-in-law was pregnant and far enough along that the ultrasound indicated she was carrying a girl.

I wasn't sure what an aardvark looked like. Maybe I saw one in a zoo. By contrast, I was certain what Aardvark, my grandchild, looked like in the dream, even though he turned into a she and she turned into a he, and they were different ages at different times during the dream. I was in charge of my grandchild's custody, and we were out and about having a good time, holding hands and walking around in a mall with a shiny floor and a food court. That's why it was so upsetting when the child disappeared. The dream cycled this disappearance a number of times.

I don't remember where we were going when I discovered the child was missing. I knew that I was responsible. The child slipped out of sight. Did I get distracted? I didn't know what happened. The realization the child was gone is what woke me up in a panic. How could I lose Aardvark? The anxiety slowly dissipated as I gained my senses.

In real life, it was only a matter of weeks until we were picking up the firstborn, Eon, as soon as my son called that he was taking my daughter-in-law to the hospital to deliver the new baby. We were on high alert. We tried to think things through. At our house, we had a pack 'n play set up, a place to change diapers, toddler-friendly food, a car seat hooked in securely in the car, etc., etc. The diaper bag would have a baby monitor, changes of clothes, and plenty of diapers and wipes. Everything was in place. We were ready.

Before Eon was born, I told my son to keep the name of their baby a secret until he was delivered. They had already decided to do so without any input from me. They knew he was a boy from the ultrasound and felt great sharing that information, even giving each set of grandparents-to-be copies of the ultrasound photo. But by keeping their baby's name to themselves, they avoided kibitzing and lobbying for any family names. They didn't need everyone's or anyone's two cents. Our son asked me for family names, but the cool names on my side of the family were taken by my older brother's and sister's kids. I called on my brother, the family genealogist, for more names, but none of the names he mentioned had any sentimental value. They followed the same game plan with this pregnancy. We had neither input nor a clue as to the name of the new baby.

We were glued to the phone after our daughter-in-law went into labor. She gave birth after a very long day. We were home rooting, praying, schvitzing (perspiring), and worrying. At one point, we were so worried that we telephoned our daughter-in-law's mother to see if she was privy to any updates. We finally heard from our son that the deed was done, and all went exceptionally well. We then first learned the name of our new grandchild: Elin Thyra Belle.

Elin is perhaps an unusual name, but I like it. I think my wife and I had our son repeat it and spell it to make sure we heard it right during that first joyous phone call. We did the same thing the first time we heard the name Eon. Maybe then we said, "Like a long time?" Maybe he said, "Yes, like that." Elin also sounded similar in a way to Eon.

It took a minute to get used to the name amidst the happiness that we felt for the healthy birthing. We said Elin and Elin Thyra Belle out loud to each other, repeating it to get used to it, similar to what we did when Eon was born.

One time, shortly after Eon was born, I must have been pretty tired when our son called to report in about the newborn. I said Enow or Ewin, something other than Eon. Well, it just popped out. My son thought I was joking. I confessed I just misspoke. I felt bad and couldn't believe I'd gotten the name wrong. I was determined not to repeat a mistake like that with Eon's new sister, Elin.

In the meantime, we needn't have worried about how things would go with Eon while his parents were at the hospital. He was having a ball, as were we. We played all the same games we played when we babysat. We read lots of books. We walked around the yard. We went to the local playground. He loved the attention, and we were intoxicated, as usual, by his happiness. We tired him out with play, and he laid down for his nap and for bed without any protest, not even a peep, the entire three days and two nights we had him.

Soon after Elin's birthing, we got to see the first picture of the new baby and her parents in the hospital, which we shared with Eon. The baby looked beautiful. I definitely liked the name Elin and felt like it went with the name Eon. Eon was also a really good-looking baby, so it appeared history had repeated itself with Elin. She looked so blissful, sleeping in the arms of her mom, with her beaming parents in the picture. Eon smiled broadly, with an expression of wonder the first time he looked at the picture of his new sister in the arms of his parents.

My dream about a gender and age-shifting grandchild named Aardvark clearly had to do with the stress of another birthing. The responsibility of taking care of Eon, and the past experience of getting used to his name, were also factors, even though I had gotten used to it very quickly and liked it very much long before I dreamed of losing Aardvark.

Eon's parents got one night at home getting situated with the new baby before we drove Eon home the next morning. They clearly missed him and couldn't wait for him to come home to meet his little sister. He acted shy and hesitant when his parents opened the door. While they greeted him with eagerness and emotion, he initially hung back at the doorway as if they were strangers. That aloofness didn't last long, as his parents hugged and kissed him anyway.

We didn't stay long, but we weren't leaving until my wife and I each got a turn holding the baby. We also got to see Eon hold the baby for the first time, bookended by his parents on the sofa. I'll never forget Eon's expression, looking at the baby and then up to his mother, speechless, sharing in his parents' joy.

IDEAS

- *Identify triggers—think about what is going to cause anxiety and brainstorm how to deal with it ahead of time.*

- *Parenting has probably changed a little since you were a parent; be open to your kids' approach with the grandkids.*

- *Stay active with one's own interests in the absence of family involvement.*

- *Give the new family space when needed and adjust your expectations.*

FRUIT AND MEALTIMES

(Luxury and Pleasure)

"Blessed are you, Lord our God, King of the Universe for there is nothing lacking in this world at all, and He created good creatures and good trees, through which pleasure is brought to the children of Adam."

TRADITIONAL SPRINGTIME PRAYER

My grandchildren always ask for more fruit, oftentimes vociferously. Their parents ask, "Is that how you ask for more?" coaxing a much calmer, "Please." These kids love raspberries, strawberries, blueberries, and grapes. Bananas, too, are great. A nice, ripe melon, mango, pear, or peach is likely to be devoured. Mandarin oranges, due to their steady availability, are an excellent go-to for a snack. The only caveat, like all foods for babies and toddlers, is to make sure every fruit is sufficiently cut up or smooshed to avoid any choking hazard.

Avocados, which Eon initially pronounced "cado," is now a familiar favorite. It took us a while to understand what he was saying the first time we heard him say, "cado." He patiently repeated himself, while his grandparents sheepishly looked at each other, drawing blanks. Luckily, a parent timely popped into the room to clear up the mystery.

Elin took a while to warm up to avocados. When first offered, when she was just starting to eat solid foods while she was still nursing, she turned away in her highchair. That was her way of saying no, and when she totally twisted around, perhaps she was saying hell no. Her parents wisely kept offering little pieces, akin to Dr. Seuss's *Sam I Am* and *Green Eggs and Ham*. Voila, one day Elin not only tried it, but discovered how much she liked it. Most times, Elin followed Eon's lead when it came to fruit and dug in.

One time, both kids were in their high chairs in the dining room when a spoon fell on the floor. The five-second rule does not apply in a house with a dog and a cat who both shed. After I ducked into the kitchen to get a clean spoon, the bowl of pineapple pieces on the table that I had been doling out to the kids was gone. Eon, who was old enough that he didn't need to be strapped into his highchair anymore, must have come halfway out of it to reach the bowl. I didn't have to ask where the pineapple went. I merely had to glance at Eon's swollen cheeks.

On a spiritual level, fruit represents abundance and pleasure. What's better than a perfectly ripe strawberry or any of the other fruits I've mentioned? Why shouldn't our youngest human beings experience sweet joy with every single bite? Why shouldn't every meal include a special, healthy treat of fresh fruit?

Fruits play an important part in cultural and religious rituals. Grapes are essential in the *Kiddush*, the sabbath and holiday blessing over the wine. Pomegranates in Judaism are alleged to contain 613 seeds representing the 613 commandments of the Torah. In Asian cultures, citruses are gifted during the Lunar New Year as a symbol of good luck and prosperity. The pineapple represents friendship and warmth in Hawaiian culture, while in Taiwan, pineapples are a symbol of wealth, independence, and good fortune. Pineapple cakes are a popular gift to tourists and native celebrants alike. Other tropical fruits, like melons, symbolize fertility and abundance due to their high water content and numerous seeds. Apples and bananas, two fruits that grow in very different climates, both connote good health. Fruit brings a richness that otherwise would not exist in the mundane fabric of everyday life. Is it any wonder that our grandkids clamor for it?

My son and daughter-in-law taught us to make sure the fruit wasn't on their plates to begin the meal; otherwise, any proteins or starches were certain to be ignored. We also learned to copy their parents' explanations at the start of each meal time, pointing and naming each food in their divided kid plates. The best technique was to leave the fruit in the other room.

This general rule about hiding the fruit does not apply to noodles. Noodles are like crack to these kids. Whether it's spaghetti, mac and cheese, or chow mein, these kids consume noodles with focus, gusto, and vigor. Speaking of starches, they also love rice. Their discovery of coconut rice at the local Thai restaurant was akin to an astronomer's discovery of Pluto.

These kids have learned to try everything, perhaps because their parents are good cooks. But their parents also live a busy urban life, where takeout delivered to the door is a delectable lifesaver with many taste choices. One night, these kids may feast on a shahi paneer and a week later sample a variety of empanadas. They don't know that they are foodies, but thanks to their parents' eclectic tastes, they are.

It is not surprising that they are also excellent restaurant kids. Their grandparents have taken them out for breakfast, lunch, and dinner. Their silicone kid plates with dividers and bibs pack easily in the diaper bag. Many places have a great kid's menu for breakfast. Many casual restaurants often offer chicken strips with fries for lunch and dinner, accompanied by the ubiquitous ranch dressing. However, these kids are just as comfortable eating sushi or lox and bagels.

There's also a Jewish mother in every grandparent who relishes when the grandchildren eat good, healthy food and is only too happy to dish out seconds. These kids are lucky to have a grandmother who has a doctorate in salmon-ology and a master's degree in matzo ball soup. She bakes and barbeques wild king or coho salmon when she wants to splurge on her kids and grandkids. Her salmon is always perfectly dressed with a little olive oil and simple spices. Utilizing her handy cooking thermometer, it comes out perfectly and is thoroughly enjoyed by all, including the munchkins.

When Grandma Donna makes matzo ball soup, a whole kosher chicken goes into a giant pot along with carrots, a parsnip, and other secret ingredients, filling the house with an aroma that connotes warmth and love. As messy as it might be for a baby and a toddler to slurp some soup, our Puget Sound winters are cold and wet, and this little "Jewish penicillin" always hits the spot.

I admire how my kids handle mealtimes with their kids. They enjoy their family mealtimes, but mealtimes are also a subtle learning opportunity. They eat together at the table. They teach basic table manners, like please and thank you. They set boundaries, too. Putting a foot on the table or banging is not allowed. Tossing food on the floor is highly discouraged. Burping for comedic effect is a no-no. They don't force their kids to eat anything, but encourage them to try everything, and they provide them repeated opportunities to taste new things. The kids get to choose what and how much to eat, but within a structure. They are not denied fruit at the end of the meal if they didn't eat or try everything. They also get snacks between mealtimes. Good job, parents! It's easy to see that eating together, with seasonal fruit at the conclusion of their meals, is a treat, a shared luxury, a daily family pleasure.

IDEAS

- *Nature's candy, fruit is a great source of vitamins, minerals, antioxidants, and fiber, a natural cancer reducer and an important part of a healthy diet. Add fruit to oatmeal, salad, smoothies, or yogurt, and make it available during the day to kids.*

- *Take kids shopping and have them pick out fruit they would like.*

- *Give them lots of choices.*

- *Arrange the fruit creatively to make the fruit appear extra special.*

LET'S ALL CLAP!

(Bonding)

"Finding true joy is the hardest of all spiritual tasks. If the only way to make yourself happy is by doing something silly, do it."

RABBI NACHMAN OF BRESLOV

A retiree might go through an average day expressionless. Getting out of bed with a self-appraisal of the pain du jour—e.g., back, neck, foot—is so routine as to occur almost unconsciously. Perhaps these aches are not easy to ignore, but you are used to them. So is your spouse. Between the two of you, whose physical problems are worse today? That's impossible to measure. Anyway, it's not a competition. Anything measuring less than seven on the pain scale isn't even worth mentioning. As stated by the great Sholem Aleichem, "No matter how bad things get, you've got to go on living, even if it kills you."

Okay, so now you're up. Pulling up the window shade, how is the weather? Cloudy, wet and cold. Duly noted. No Tsunami, hurricane, or forest fire smoke in the air. The weather, whether wet or dry, might feel hum-drum. Not something to get excited about today.

Jumping on the scale in the bathroom confirms that grazing the kitchen pantry after dinner, yet again, was a bad idea.

Time to take the dog out and pick up its poo. In the process, you note the weeds in the garden haven't stopped growing. In fact, the worst ones, the horsetails, appear to be gathering momentum, as if they are gathering to attend a yearly convention.

Time for the same-old-same-old breakfast? Drinking coffee always helps, but looking at what's new in the news tamps down any lift from the caffeine. The latest sensationalistic tidbit of news doesn't even raise an eyebrow. You are feeling the malaise of another day in retirement.

A taciturn expression is the norm. This malaise is not depression; it's reality. Another day hung over from the last night's latest television binge. No reason to frown. No reason to smile. Nothing tickling your laugh button; nothing tickling your fancy.

But then appears a little hint of an inner smiley feeling in the midst of this robotic routine. Today is a grandparent day. We, the grandparents, are the daycare. Departure in about an hour for a drive to visit the grandkids, the precious babies! Instantly, the mood changes. What can we bring them this time? Time to peek in the basement storage container of old stuff. Quick, grab a new, old book and another new, old matchbook car. Nothing like a little gift to start the visit.

The miserable drive with the inevitable traffic jams won't last forever. Remember what little Eon said when we arrived last time? "Oh, Gwandma, I missed you so much!" That little *mensch*! What a charmer! We arrive and find a parking space near the rental. Someone sees you through the picture window! Your favorite two-and-a-half-year-old. He is jumping up and down on the sofa, an ebullient greeting.

When the doors open, a little holding back, a moment of shyness, but then the surprise of that loveliest of sentiments again, "Oh Gwandma, I missed you so much!" Maybe he remembered the positive, heartfelt response the first time he said it and wanted to gauge the reaction again. Then, before Grandma Donna could even take her shoes off, "I'm playing cars!" and a dash into the family room.

Big smiles greet the seven-month-old baby, who is held up high to facilitate your greeting, "Hi baby! Hi little Elin!" Mwah, a kiss on the forehead, says Grandma. Hugs and how are you, how's it going, to the nanny who has to leave. Within minutes, you are holding the baby. You are told that little Elin has started to smile more, but you are going to have to work for yours. Her expression may at first say, "Who are you?" or "Where's mom?" Grandma's expression, in contrast, is animated with smiles and goofy faces, with all semblance of dignity thrown to the wind. After some healthy mugging, "Look, I got a smile!" exclaims Grandma.

Over time, Grandma's silliness pays off. Elin, at age one-and-one-half, and Grandma Donna, at age we won't say, have a go-to game of funny faces they usually play every get-together. They purse their lips, they raise their eyebrows, they frown. Elin laughs when Grandma Donna and I fake cry.

Big brother's go-to is playing cars with me. "Hi," says the race car. "Hi. I'm red race car." "Hi, I'm yellow car." "Hi, I'm the po-po (police)." "Hi." "Hi."

Our stiffness, aches, and pains haven't gone away, but they recede like a king tide going out fast.

In contrast to our early morning malaise, we spend our visiting hours exercising all our facial muscles. Our reserved expressions give way to smiling, laughing, shaking heads up and down and to and fro. Sometimes, we frown, repeat "No throwing," raise our eyebrows, and imitate various animal sounds, choo-choo trains, and sleeping noises while playing and reading books with both kids.

When a baby laughs at her older brother, who is making faces and monkey sounds for his sister, the whole world laughs. Is there anything that adds joy to life faster than a grandchild's laugh? It frees the mind and fills the soul with flowers the colors of the rainbow.

Any of the baby's first words bring sheer joy. Food words are prime vocabulary. Elin is a good eater. She knows how to say, "Mor!" when it comes to the cut-up pieces of strawberries she finds so delicious. Her older brother agrees. "Do you want more, too, Eon?" "So many!" he replies.

Sometimes, it's all about what makes them laugh. Eon wants the alligator puppet with the big rubber mouth that's currently on my hand to eat what Eon puts in its mouth, but everything falls out. Finally, I hold the alligator upside down so the things in its mouth stay in. Eon's approval is confirmed with his squealing laughter. Eon's disapproval is also apparent. He becomes quiet when the puppet is fighting with the stuffed animal. I notice. "You don't like fighting, do you, Eon?"

"I," (slight pause), "do," (slight pause), "not," he replies.

We repeat every new word the baby says. One of her favorite words is Eon. Another is book. Sometimes, she says, "Mama," when Mom isn't around. She is missing her mother, but we reassure with, "Mom will be home soon," or, "Mom's at work," said matter-of-factly.

Eon wants to push all the buttons on my swim watch. The watch has three black buttons and one orange button. The orange button lights up the watch face, while the black buttons control the alarm, stopwatch, and the date and time functions. I let him push the orange button, but not the black buttons. Of course, Eon wants to know why. I tell him that Grandma Donna doesn't like to hear the alarm sounds. Of course, he wants to know why she doesn't like the alarm sounds. He thinks it's so funny when he's told the alarm sounds make Grandma crazy, that he repeats it over and over, and it becomes a game.

"Don't pwess the black buttons," he tells me, "They drive Gwandma cwazy!"

He pushes the orange button repeatedly and enjoys the joke when he thinks of it sitting next to me eating at the table, reading books, or getting into the stroller. The same joke is repeated often over a number of visits. Eon loves to push buttons on my watch, to end a video call, or to call an elevator.

Elin loves peekaboo when we put on or take off her sweatshirt to go out to the store or the playground.

"Where's Elin?" we ask, pausing while her head and eyes are covered. "There she is!" we say when she can see us again. She says, "sock," when we put on her socks.

Nap time is preceded by a little cuddling and reading some books. Elin cries just a little when put down for her nap, but not for long. Grandma Donna tells me not to worry about it, that she will settle down, and she does. Who wouldn't object to leaving a grandmother's warm embrace for a flat, inanimate surface?

Eon puts up a little fight. "I won't sleep," or "I'm not tired," he says, although he will sleep and is clearly tired. When he wakes up, he is quick to say, "I didn't sleep! I only wested."

Elin soon calls or cries to tell us she's awake, too. Maybe they'd like a little snack.

When Mom or Dad arrives home from work, there's a lot of excitement. "Mama!" "Dada!" We can pass the torch. It's always fun to eat dinner together before taking off. The highlight is when everyone laughs, and Elin smiles and claps her hands. Eon notices and says, "Let's all clap!" Elin laughs and claps some more, along with everyone clapping, laughing, and smiling.

What are we clapping about? We're just clapping because Elin clapped, and Eon said, "Let's all clap." We all join in the fun.

The drive home is a grind, but not too bad. It was a great day.

IDEAS

- *Make your grandchild a memory book that tells your life story. There are many how-to memory books available with guided prompts and places to add photos.*

- *Make a scrapbook with your grandchildren about their activities and field trips.*

- *Visit your grandchildren as often as you can!*

- *Help them help you make breakfast.*

- *Share your special skills and hobbies.*

- *Plan special outings with your grandkids, such as to the park, aquarium, zoo, or the local bakery or ice cream parlor.*

SWEET PEAS

(Gardening)

*"To forget how to dig the earth and to tend the
soil is to forget ourselves."*

MAHATMA GANDHI

My daughter-in-law has a tight group of girlfriend graduates from
medical school who have scattered far and wide, but they get together
each Spring to enjoy an out-of-town reunion, dragging their spouses
along. The other grandparents were on a road trip—were we available
to take the kids? You bet! We would be delighted. We were excited to get
both of our grandkids for five days.

When we checked the dates, Grandma Donna decided to cancel her
8 a.m. weight-lifting classes, but we didn't know what to do about my two
physical therapy appointments, also both at 8 a.m. I was recovering from
a fractured and dislocated shoulder that required an open reduction
and internal fixation surgery; in other words, a plate and pins. We
decided that I shouldn't miss therapy appointments that were hard to
schedule.

We knew from experience that wake-up time was a prime and very
busy time for caring for a one-year-old and a three-year-old. They both

liked to read books when they woke up. Then there was the diaper changing, getting dressed, a little energetic playing, and breakfast. They let us know when they awoke. The baby, little Elin, usually gave a little *geshrey* (cry), while Eon, the three-year-old, called, "Grandma, I'm up! I'm up, Grandma Donna!" Wake-up time meant, ready or not, we had to shake off the cobwebs and get on with it.

We asked my brother-in-law, who lived a half-day's drive away, if he'd like to come visit to help out and hang out for the extended sleepover. He hadn't had much time with the kids and he said yes. That calmed our grandparent nerves, knowing we'd have an extra pair of hands and eyes to help out, especially as one of my arms couldn't pick up the kids during wake-up and meal times.

Three-year-old Eon was very interested in my shoulder "owie." He frequently asked to see the scar. He probably remembered visiting before surgery, when I wore a simple sling, and seeing me after surgery in an immobilizer, a fancy-looking sling with a foam pillow. He remembered his parents told him not to bang into Grandy's "owie" when we read books together.

One-plus-year-old Elin was very interested in opening drawers and going up and down steps, but our insecurity caused us to repeatedly remind her to go down the steps backwards, even though she probably didn't need reminding. She changed directions as she approached the steps, whether we reminded her or not. But it's one of those things you can't help saying.

The kids got more familiar with Uncle Rich, who acquired the name Uncle Ritzi, and he with them. Having three adults took all the pressure off watching the kids while preparing the meals, changing a diaper, or taking our dogs out.

Uncle Ritzi thoroughly enjoyed the kids. We went to the zoo, turned over rocks on a saltwater pebble beach to look for little crabs, and threw rocks in the water. We read books. We played cars, Brio trains, imaginary cooking, and shot basketballs into the little hoop with the mini-basketballs. One day, we went to the library to check out books and to a Mexican restaurant for cheese quesadillas, beans, and rice.

One game that we invented went on for a long time. It was called Hall Ball. We took the mini-basketballs and a small beach ball and went into the hallway. We closed the doors to the bedrooms and laundry room, leaving us with a long hallway where the balls stayed in play. Grandma Donna sat on the floor on one end, and Elin sat on my lap down at the other end of the long hallway. Eon ran up and back as we and he tossed the balls back and forth. Eon signaled his enjoyment by jumping up and down following any particularly exciting throw, or when one ball careened off another. Elin also enjoyed throwing the balls, which she barely managed with her two little arms and hands.

Elin had one bad night when she woke up with what Grandma Donna called a tummy-tutu. She cried big sobs, and her stomach seemed tight. She felt warm. With a lot of comforting, she was able to get back to sleep relatively quickly. We didn't resort to any medication.

She also smashed her finger closing a kitchen drawer, which caused a silent scream followed by a big cry. As the cries subsided, she wanted her mama, but she had to make do with us. She recovered quickly with our comforting. Another time, we expected a major injury when she stumbled and fell face-first on the driveway, but her hands broke her fall, and she got up without even a peep. Stoic Elin!

Eon was a good communicator. He protested nap time and bedtime by calmly stating that he wouldn't sleep. But sleep he did, although he denied it when he woke up. It was obvious he had dozed off by his disheveled hair and puffy-looking face.

One time, after a morning diaper change, Eon slipped off the bed, which was serving as a diaper changing table, and climbed into Elin's pack 'n play, which was borrowed from the other grandparents and was serving as her crib. Eon jumped up and down like it was a trampoline, which also bounced Elin all around, much to the amusement of both of them. Grandma Donna, on the other hand, was not amused, because the jumping and bouncing not only looked like an injury waiting to happen to the baby, but also because the pack 'n play wasn't ours. Eon's jumping shook it enough that Grandma Donna thought it might rip or tear. She left Eon in the pack 'n play to jump around while scooping up Elin to change her diaper. Both kids laughed their heads off while she took care of Elin.

Grandma Donna's entreaties to Eon to hop out were met with repeated giggles and "noes" of varying volume. After repeated requests, she resorted to her superior physical size and strength, but the youngster had suddenly developed an ability to squirm out of her grasp. The game not only continued, but it got better as Eon squealed with delight each time he evaded her grasp. Grandma Donna's frustration was magnified when I poked my head into the room with a weak, "What's going on?" Uncle Ritzi was nowhere to be found.

Finally, Grandma Donna, surprising herself, was able to grab Eon with lightning-quick hands, yank him out, and gently let him down onto the floor. He wasn't happy about it, but he didn't pout for more than a second and certainly didn't hold a grudge. He was simply at that age where, occasionally, he had to assert his independence. Later, Grandma Donna reflected that she shouldn't have let a power struggle develop, but I'm not sure what her alternative might have been. This was the only actual disagreement during the entire five-day visit, other than Eon's protests when it was time for bed.

The visit also coincided with the perfect time to start my yearly vegetable garden. The garden was a big question mark for the first time ever due to my surgery. Uncle Ritzi came to the rescue. He did yeoman's work to prepare the garden beds. He got down on his knees, broke up the dirt, and pulled out the weeds. He used my favorite tool, a CobraHead, a weeder with a boomerang curve of metal and a spade on the end, to plow and weed the raised beds. Eon and Elin also helped pull out a weed or two. They enjoyed the feel of the dirt. Eon and Elin helped spread some mushroom compost with little handfuls at a time. Eon then helped Grandy sweep out the greenhouse. While Grandy did the sweeping, Eon held the dustbin and carried the debris to the lawn.

When Uncle Ritzi finished prepping the garden bed, it was time to plant the first seeds of the year, the peas. Peas can handle a little cold weather. We made little grooves with our index fingers in the soil for Eon and Elin to plant the peas. Eon and Elin carefully placed the peas where we pointed to adequately space them. Once we had all the peas in place, they helped cover them up and pat down the soil.

Elin lost interest in the peas and busied herself with some rocks in the gravel driveway. We found an old bucket so she could put the rocks there rather than in the garden bed. Eon found some big landscaping rocks nearby and joined Elin, putting the big rocks in the bucket. When we watered the peas, the kids wanted water in their bucket, so the rocks splashed when they dropped in. That was great fun, as was watching the dogs drink water from the hose. If Grandma Donna hadn't called for lunchtime, we'd all still be there, plopping rocks into the bucket.

When the pea seedlings pop out of the ground, I hope Eon and Elin will come and visit and remember when they planted the seeds. This year's garden is special, because it might not have even happened without Uncle Ritzi's help. And he wouldn't have been around, but for Eon and Elin. They may be little, but they cause such good things to happen.

You could say gardening is in my blood. I've had a garden every year for over four decades. I hope my grandkids take to gardening like I did. According to Genesis, humankind's first task was to tend to the Garden of Eden. It is always good for the soul to plant a vegetable garden. Prepping the beds and planting the first seeds of Spring is invariably a good feeling. How much more so with peas tenderly planted by Eon and Elin? Seeds represent potential, as do our grandchildren. Grandma Donna calls these kids our little sweet peas.

CONSIDER

- *Create a garden with your grandkids: pea seeds are big enough for little hands to grasp and plant, radishes grow fast, and cherry tomatoes are easy to pick.*

- *Encourage them to dig around in the soil.*

- *Take kids on a worm hunt!*

- *Grow pumpkins. You can save them for Halloween!*

STOP, LOOK BOTH WAYS

(Child Safety)

"Just as a person is obligated to teach their child, so it is their duty to teach their grandchildren, as it says, 'Make them known to your children, and to your children's children.'"

DEUT. 4:9

A rule is a rule when it comes to safety. Even when your grandchild is in the stroller and doesn't yet walk, we announce what we're doing. She's in a stroller, but we stop. We look both ways. We tell her we are stopping and looking both ways. We take pains to do this even when there is absolutely no traffic. Why? She can't talk yet, but she can hear, and we can communicate basic safety at this tender age. We like to train the neuro-pathways as soon as possible. A parent and grandparent must ensure the child's safety. The child's safety is forever present in our consciousness.

It wasn't long after Eon and Elin learned to walk that they each learned to run. Looking at it from their point of view, why walk when you can run—especially when you can bring your toy or book from the other room to show me or Grandma Donna? Running at that early toddler age is an expression of exuberance, excitement, physicality, and fun. Do they appreciate the risk of falling? They fell many times in the process of learning to walk and run, but in the moment that they are dashing here and there, they aren't thinking about it. They just like to run.

When your grandchildren are old enough to take a walk with you outside the house, and also at an age where they enjoy running around for the sheer pleasure of it, they must learn to stop, look both ways, walk, not run, and hold hands to cross the street. He or she may not want to hold hands, but it's a rule. Even before age three, they reflexively learn to grab your hand as you come to the end of the block. Looking both ways and holding hands becomes automatic, internalized somewhere around age two. And what parent or grandparent doesn't enjoy holding that little person's hand? What little person doesn't enjoy holding a parent or grandparent's hand? The simple act of touch, of connectedness, does much to alleviate fears.

What is possibly different in today's world, but absolutely merits mention, is a scary and sensitive subject—child sexual abuse and exploitation, any parent's nightmare. I distinctly remember my mom drilling into our heads when we were little kids, "Don't talk to strangers." I wondered why, because she was friendly and outgoing to people she didn't know. She talked to strangers. I was very shy, and I didn't want to talk to strangers, which she had to know, so that compounded my wonder about her admonition.

I also remember that she said never to get into the car of someone I didn't know, even if they offered me candy. I couldn't imagine getting into someone's car if I didn't know them, and how weird it would be if someone I didn't know offered me candy (and I wasn't trick or treating on Halloween). But I appreciated that Mom was laying down a stern and serious rule simply by her tone.

Perhaps in those days, people thought that a sexual predator was a weirdo who pulled up in a car with candy, or someone who wore a dark raincoat and hung out in the alley. I know from my criminal lawyer days that it doesn't happen like that. The pedophile is more likely a family member, family friend, or the local priest or minister who engages in grooming behavior over a period of time. What Mom told me way back when, as well-intentioned as it was, doesn't cut it in today's world. So, what do you tell your grandchildren, and when do you tell them?

There must also be a balance between securing your child or grandchild's safety and not instilling paralyzing fear. The child development psychologists posit four messages to calmly convey to young children as follows:[12]

1. No one should tell you to keep secrets from Mom and Dad.
2. Your body is yours and belongs to you.
3. There is good and bad touching. You don't touch anyone, and no one touches you, in the area where you wear a bathing suit, unless it's a doctor and Mom or Dad are in the room.
4. No one has the right to make you feel uncomfortable.

I don't know what the statistics were back in the 1950s or 60s, when I was a little kid, or even if they kept statistics then. But the estimates

---

12 Lena Aburdene Derhally, "How to talk to kids about sexual abuse, and how you can help prevent it," *The Washington Post*, February 8, 2017, https://www.washingtonpost.com/news/parenting/wp/2017/02/08/how-to-talk-to-kids-about-sexual-abuse-and-how-you-can-help-prevent-it/.

now are hair-raising. The CDC (Centers for Disease Control) posits that approximately one in four girls and one in six boys are sexually abused in childhood.[13] The U.S. Department of Justice has estimated that only 10 percent of the perpetrators were strangers to the victim, and 23 percent of the perpetrators were children.

Experts say that little kids should be free to talk about body parts, and we should use the correct anatomical names when these conversations come up. The four rules listed above can be naturally worked into these talks. These conversations should let the kids know that these rules also apply to other kids and adults they know, not just strangers. Kids should also know that they can tell parents and grandparents about anything they feel weird about, and they will never be in trouble, even if they were told not to tell or that something was a secret. No one wants to think about child sexual abuse, let alone talk about it. It is a difficult subject, but let's follow some expert advice and subtly give our little ones some common sense tools to avoid trauma and victimization.

Fear is part of the human condition. Little kids are going to be afraid of things like loud, startling noises, the dark, certain bugs, snakes or animals, or maybe even imaginary monsters at different points in their development. The best thing we can do as grandparents is create a safe place so they can tell you what they are worried about. You may have to play detective when they are really little and don't have the language skills to tell you what's bugging them.

There was a time when Eon kept crawling around and looking in the corners of a room near the fireplace, and we couldn't figure out

13 Centers for Disease Control, "Preventing Child Abuse and Neglect," May 16, 2024, https://www.cdc.gov/child-abuse-neglect/prevention/index.html.

what he was doing. Finally, we found out from Mom and Dad that he was inspecting for spider webs and spiders. I liked that his parents were neither encouraging nor, more importantly, discouraging his search for spiders. They were letting him deal with it, giving him control of the situation by inspecting for spiders in the corners.

Child psychologists say that validating rather than dismissing fears, and letting kids work through particular fears at their own pace, is the way to go.[14] The toddler may crash his cars but then fly them to the hospital, where they quickly get better with a magic, imaginary shot from another car that is a make-believe doctor. Lots of fears get worked out in play. Also, many children's books address all sorts of fears about real things, like scary animals or insects, or imaginary things, like monsters.

One child may really benefit from a nightlight or the door cracked open a tad, while the other wants it pitch dark. It's nice to have a special blanket or stuffed animal to help with separation anxiety at bedtime. Some say that the ubiquitous peek-a-boo game addresses the child's fear of a parent going away, demonstrating the parent's return. Routines and games help a great deal to alleviate fears.

I can't tell you how many times, as parents, my wife and I told our kids to be careful. Maybe we overdid it. You don't want your kids to be overcautious, but it was in our DNA to say, "Be careful!" over and over again. Apparently, they somehow survived our overprotectiveness. It is hard as a parent to strike the right balance.

---

14 Shana B. Diskant, "How Parents Can Validate Kids' Feelings," *Psychology Today,* March 29, 2022, https://www.psychologytoday.com/us/blog/the-adjustment-adjunct/202203/how-parents-can-validate-kids-feelings.

Hopefully, we can hold ourselves back from overdoing it as grand-parents. We want to instill a consciousness of safety without creating unnecessary anxieties. In other words, humans of all ages need to let our fears prevent us from dangers or unreasonable risks without giving in to irrational fears. If we are scared of heights or suffer a fear of flying, as examples, we don't have to share that by acting out or going on and on about it in front of the grandkids. If the subject comes up, we can freely admit what scares us, but not in a way that teaches them they need to share that fear. If they are lucky enough to enjoy a view from a high overlook or go on an airplane as a toddler, we want them to thoroughly enjoy their experience rather than meltdown with fear.

Grandchildren are such a gift. We can escape from our turbulent times when we immerse ourselves in the innocent world of wonder and curiosity that comes so naturally to our grandchildren. Grandparenting is uplifting fun, but also an enormous responsibility. We want to nurture and care for these little, precious human beings. We want to protect them and keep them safe. At the same time, we don't want them to live in fear. We want to impart good habits and attitudes.

In our most mature years, perhaps we have been so clobbered by our own fears that we are conditioned to really focus on selfish needs. Perhaps we have lost touch with that free, inner child deep inside us. When we get out of ourselves in the presence of our grandchildren, to rediscover the innocent joy and spontaneity they possess, we also intuitively care about their safety and well-being. We create a protective cocoon. That allows our grandchildren to develop their true personalities and capabilities. In so doing, we are careful not to run away from what we're scared of and, most importantly, what scares them.

IDEAS

- *It may seem obvious, but keep sharp objects such as knives or needles out of reach—same for hot food.*

- *Cover electric sockets in your home when kids come to visit.*

- *Help kids memorize or write down important numbers in case of an emergency.*

- *Use gates to help keep toddlers in safe places, like away from stairs.*

FURTHER READING

See, "Tip Sheet: The Unique Role of Grandparents in Preventing Child Sexual Abuse," *See,* https://www.stopitnow.org/ohc-content/tip-sheet-the-unique-role-of-grandparents-in-preventing-child-sexual-abuse

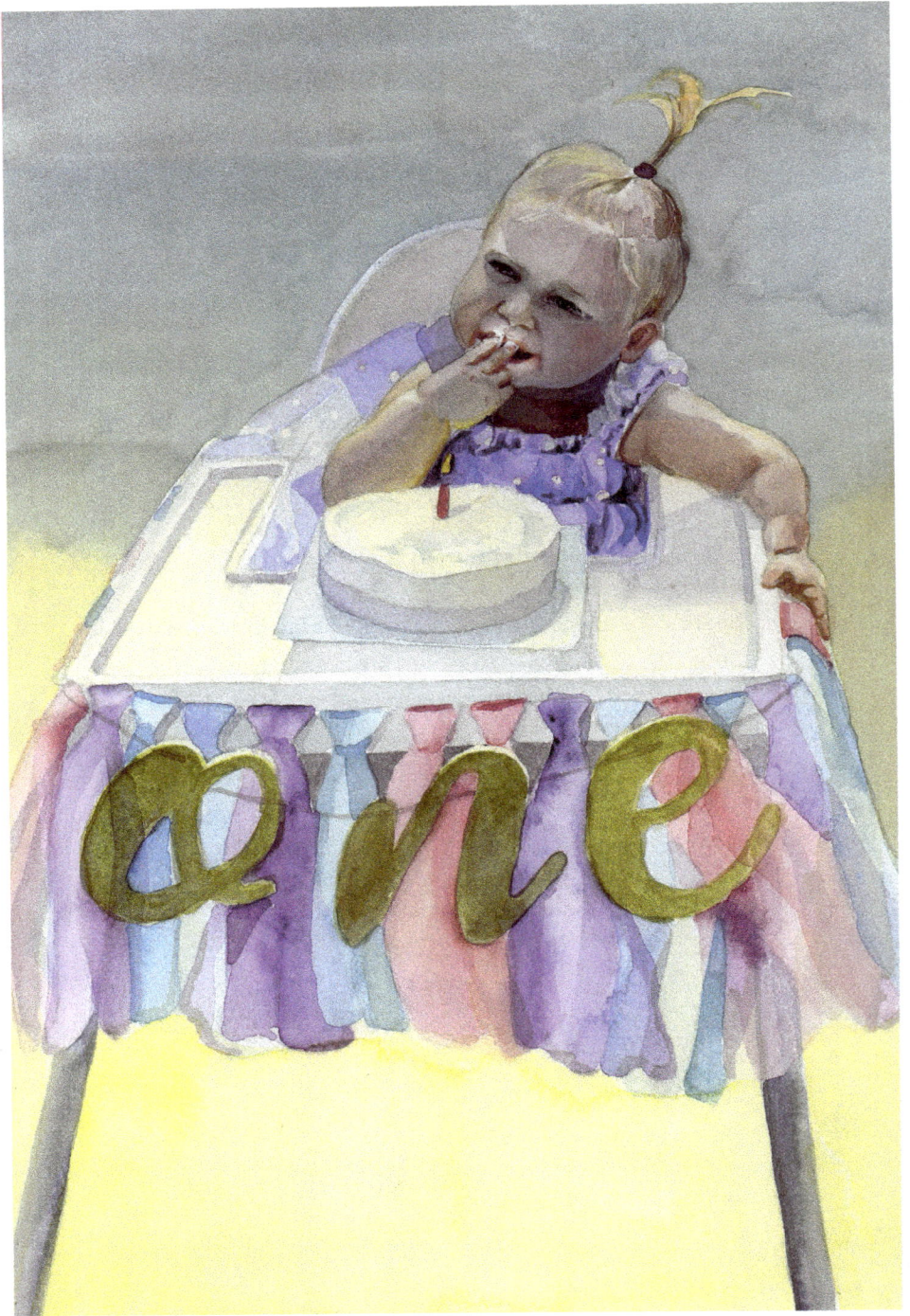

THE SEVENTIETH BIRTHDAY

(Aging)

"At five years of age the study of Scripture; At ten the study of Mishnah; At thirteen subject to the commandments; At fifteen the study of Talmud; At eighteen the bridal canopy; At twenty for pursuit [of livelihood]; At thirty the peak of strength; At forty wisdom; At fifty able to give counsel; At sixty old age; At seventy fullness of years; At eighty the age of "strength"; At ninety a bent body; At one hundred, as good as dead and gone completely out of the world."

PIRKEI AVOT (ETHICS OF THE FATHERS), 5:21

I never thought much about birthdays. I took them in stride. Looking back, thirteen was putting the Bar Mitzvah in the rear-view mirror, with the promise from Mom that I wouldn't have to go to Sunday School any longer. Sixteen meant a driver's license, but you had to pass the driver's test with the tight-lipped DMV person. Twenty-one meant I could officially drink, which my friends and I had practiced for years, but now we could go into a bar. At thirty, I was inexperienced, wet behind the ears, but up and coming at work. My nose was to the grindstone. I was sincerely ambitious and wanted to please. At forty, I had hit my stride and had more work than I could handle.

At fifty, I was in my prime, starting my power years and celebrating a jubilee year to boot. Contemporaneously, my fifties were a mixed bag. I became an orphan in my fifties, losing both parents, who were elderly and ill. I didn't want them to suffer, but still, anytime you lose a parent, it is a heavy loss. These losses were ameliorated by the progress of our young children, and how busy each member of the family continued to be during those years.

In my mid-sixties, with kids off at college, I could look back on accomplishments in my life with some sense of achievement, but what about that pesky thing called aging? Wasn't I getting up there? I preferred not to think about birthdays in my sixties, because every year in my sixties was bringing me closer to the dreaded seventies.

You can say age is just a number, but to me, seventy meant O L D. As a longtime sports fan, I know that you cannot cheat Father Time. Aging in sports definitely meant diminished performance, and if you didn't retire, soon you were booted from the team. What did age seventy mean to me?

I was in denial about my seventieth birthday throughout my sixties. True, my late sixties meant a desired retirement: time to read and write, more time to garden, without feeling as rushed, time to travel on fun trips with my wife, and time to relax. Wonderful things happened in my sixties, not the least of which was my children earning advanced degrees, honors, and independence. Each kid became a real mensch; still kids to me, but clearly adults to the world at large. In my sixties, I started writing books, which opened up a new world of learning. I wrote five books and published four paperbacks and three audiobooks.

When I gave talks about my books, my audience was often an older crowd. I pandered to their agedness by critiquing our contemporary society's lionization of the young, the new and the shiny. I borrowed from Judaic principles to compare the human experience to that of a tree of the field. A tree is at its most magnificent when fully mature. I asked the audience if they valued seniority or inferiority, maturity or immaturity. I relied on biblical precepts and proverbs, extolling the virtues of the wisdom that comes with age and greater experience.

Yet, and perhaps hypocritically, I didn't internalize what I preached. I felt an unease about aging. My birthdays during my sixties whispered in my ear like a ghost haunting me, reminding me of my own mortality. A few friends and colleagues passed away. In several cases, the deaths came as real shocks. I loyally attended memorial services and sincerely grieved the loss of three friends with whom I was very close. Each death sent me for a loop.

Even though I was eating healthier and dedicating more time to exercising in my sixties, it was undeniable that my physical health was on the decline. Ice, Biofreeze, a heating pad, and ibuprofen were each frequent go-tos. When it came to walking, bending, or lifting, I simply couldn't do as much without significant pains and restrictions. I had some injuries and flare-ups, and my day-to-day was interrupted by periods of significant pain, mild disability, and repeated trips to a wonderfully positive and helpful physical therapist. My wife's frequent refrain was to not overdo it. The kids echoed the same message.

All of this is to say, I was really dreading my seventieth birthday. My adult kids were insistent that we celebrate it, despite my sharing the desire to entirely avoid the subject. When pressed for a second or third time, I told them that the only thing I'd like for my birthday was a family sleepover with the grandkids.

Arrangements were made, and the day arrived. How was it? Well, it was like when you don't want to go to a party, and then you go and have a great time. We were blessed with wonderful weather and spent the time outside. We planted sunflower seeds, put rocks in a bucket of water, looked for baby crabs on the beach, where we turned over rock after rock, and then we enjoyed our grandkids playing in the sprinklers.

We had a fun birthday dinner. After we sang "Happy Birthday" and ate cheesecake, made by my wife from a tried-and-true family recipe, we went around the table and sang silly made-up songs that mostly rhymed. The next morning, Elin sang her own rendition of "Happy Birthday" in the sweetest sing-song imaginable by a one-and-one-half-year-old. My son and daughter-in-law gave me a white ballcap colored with magic marker squiggles of all sorts drawn by my two grandkids.

Contrast a seventieth birthday with a baby's first birthday. A birthday for a one-year-old is a family celebration of the new baby and all the joy she has brought. Parents might dress up the baby and let her sit in her highchair and go to town on her personalized birthday cake, lovingly made from scratch by her mom. It is certainly a time to get together to share the jubilation and gratitude everyone feels for this newest member of the family.

A birthday for a two-year-old or a three-year-old is a celebration of the transition from babyhood to toddlerhood to preschooler—and all the developmental milestones the youngster is achieving. My mother often told the story that my three-year-old birthday was a breakthrough of sorts. I told everyone, "I'm fwee; I talk now."

My general critique of birthday parties, at the risk of sounding like a curmudgeon, is not the celebration of the birthday boy or girl, but how we go about it. While we want to feed our youngsters a healthy diet, on their birthdays, we overload them (and ourselves) with sugar. While we want to instill in our kids real conscientiousness and caring values, on their birthdays, we indoctrinate them into an orgy of materialism, showering them with lots of stuff wrapped in fancy paper and ribbons.

I'm all for little kids' birthdays, a special day where the child is celebrated. She and her parents can feel connected to their closest family members and friends. But it can be tough for a typically shy little one to be in a big spotlight. Not everyone shines as the center of attention at age one, two or three. It's also stressful for the parent(s). My best advice is to take a deep breath or several. Ask the child about a theme for the party, and then have fun with the decorations without overdoing it. Keep the food simple. Time it right to coincide with nap schedules.

I've read about elaborate and pricey little kid parties at rented venues, with over-the-top decorations, ice sculptures, rented entertainers, fancy party-favor bags, and long guest lists. Don't do it. Not necessary! And it sends the wrong message to the child about what is important. We can have a happy birthday with connectedness, celebration, gratitude, and love, without all the rest. It's not how much you plan, spend, and stress. It's a mom remembering someone saying, "I'm fwee; I talk now." It's my wife and I hearing a smiling one-and-one-half-year-old Elin singing her version of "Happy Birthday" the next day. She sang, "Happy, happy…happy, happy…"

BIRTHDAY IDEAS

- *Provide a fun home activity like easy arts and crafts for the whole family.*

- *Have squirt gun wars (on a hot summer day) or an outdoor movie night.*

- *Take kids out to a farm or a petting zoo and meet the animals!*

- *Let kids create a special food menu or pick a theme for decorations for their birthday party!*

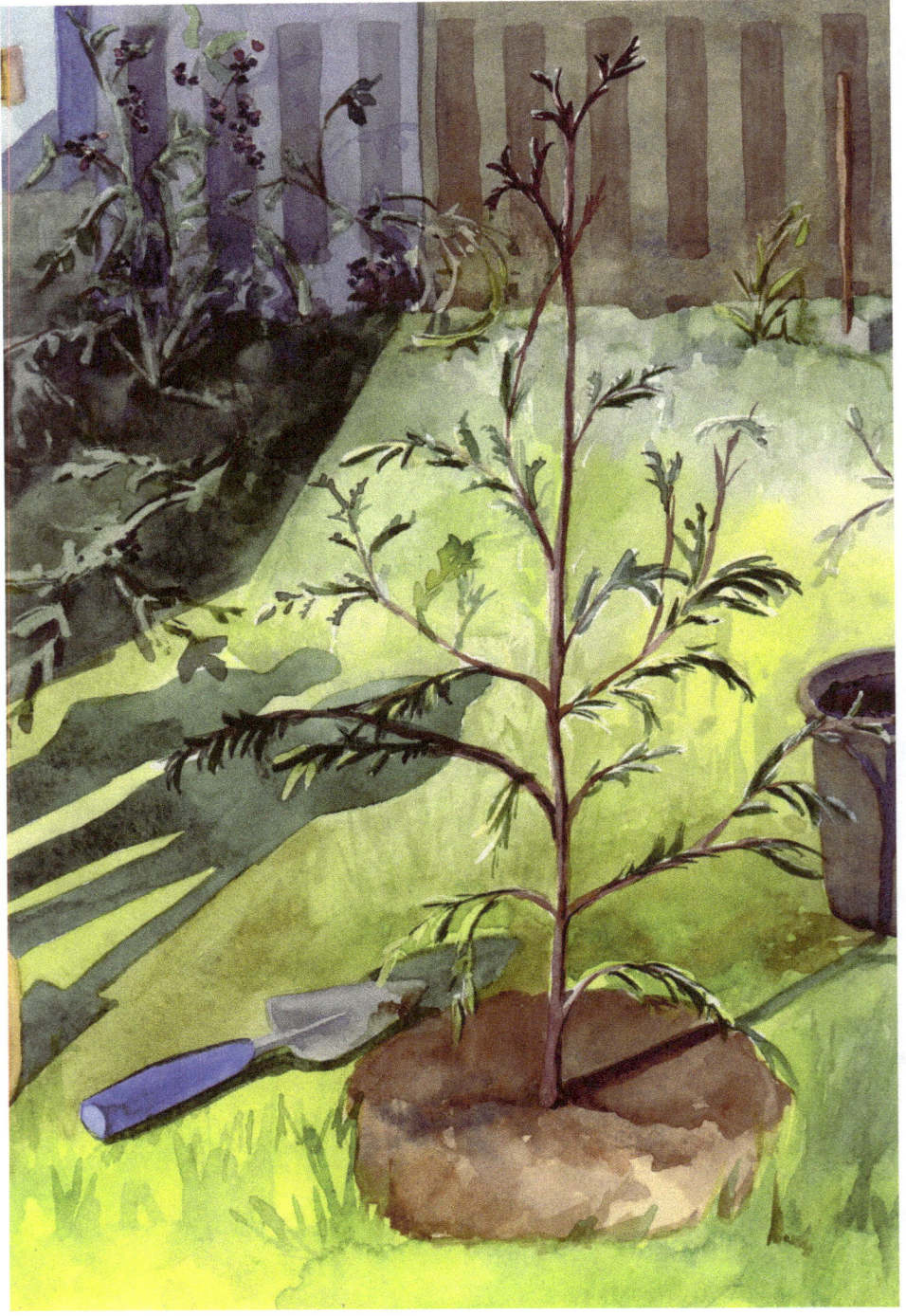

EON'S FOREST

(Planting Trees)

"The true meaning of life is to plant trees, and create shade where you do not necessarily expect to sit."

KAMARI A.K.A. LYRIKAL

It was only natural for me to clear a section of our yard next to a saltwater inlet that was overgrown with invasive blackberry bushes choking out other natural flora. It wasn't easy. A long-neglected, overgrown thicket of berry bushes and vines is prickly, intertwined, and stubbornly rooted to the spot. Even with a long-sleeved shirt, you are bound to get scratched up. We huddled up after a failed attempt at clearing the blackberries. We thought about how to attack the mess without getting scratched. We bought special gloves that go up your arms past your wrists, and we wore heavy, long-sleeved shirts and thick pants to minimize the pricks and scratches. We pulled and yanked and cut and raked until we had two piles of vines that filled three beds of a pick-up truck. Even after all that, we could still see where the plants had firmly rooted into the ground.

A number of folks told us we'd have to spray one of the poisons that is heavily advertised and available in the big box stores to really stop the blackberries from growing back. But we found spraying a high concentration of vinegar just where each plant rooted did the trick. You could see that it worked by the next day, when the plants that were left dried out and died.

We don't like to use commercial weed killers and fertilizers, especially when we live on an inlet of the Salish Sea that is alive with marine life. We also have a fenced yard with dogs and vegetable beds. We don't want the dogs rolling around in stuff coated with toxic chemicals. Most importantly, we have children and little grandchildren who like to play outside when they visit. We care about human health, including our own and those close to us, as much as the health of the environment. Why take unneeded risks by spraying chemicals that kill the plants and remains in the dirt we frequent?

We were very happy that the concentrated vinegar solution, which you can make yourself, buy online, or surprisingly also find in the gardening chain stores, worked really well. We were also pleased to spare the Oregon grape and pickleweed, two native plants that we uncovered in the thick of the blackberry vines.

What does any of this have to do with grandparenthood? We were already calling this plot of waterfront ground Eon's Forest. I had a vision of a healthy plot of native trees and shrubs instead of a mess of invasive, prickly bushes. Naming the plot Eon's Forest served as the inspiration to remove the nasty thickets of blackberries. Sometimes, a little extra motivation really helps tackle the hard gardening jobs. Thinking of your grandchildren can really provide that extra needed oomph.

Since the space we cleared lent itself to planting several trees, we could tell Eon that this area would become a mini-forest planted in his honor. He could watch the trees grow as he grew. I also imagined Eon experiencing the fun of planting his own little native tree—helping to dig the hole, transferring the sapling, filling dirt in around the roots, and setting the sapling at just the right height. I knew he would love watering it in for the very first time. Planting a native tree at the right time in the right place is always a fun activity.

Naming this area Eon's Forest would also inspire us to maintain and improve the area with native plants, and keep out the non-native plants, as the little tree saplings grew. Spray as we might with the vinegar, the blackberries had been embedded for so long that some of the stubbornly-rooted plants were certain to return.

I'm a longtime gardener in the Pacific Northwest. When weeding, I frequently find tiny cedar and fir seedlings that I carefully transfer to a container and take care to water during the hottest months. They are big enough that after a few years of growth, they are ready to plant or give away. Accordingly, I had plenty of seedlings to choose from to replace the blackberry patch.

Coincidentally, I saw a flier online for an upcoming talk from a master gardener who had studied the Miyawaki method of reforestation. Miyawaki was a master botanist who studied forests adjacent to Shinto shrines and developed reforestation plans for smaller areas that involved native trees, shrubs, and ground coverings. Never had I imagined that something akin to my vision for Eon's Forest had already been studied, designed, and developed as a famous method of reforestation. I learned that Miyawaki had planted an amazing amount of trees in this way in fifteen countries, in addition to Japan. He specialized in turning what he termed ecological deserts into thriving, biodiverse native forests and gardens.

Planting and caring for trees enjoys a lengthy, spiritual tradition in Judaism. In the first chapter of the Old Testament, God tells Adam to cultivate and guard the trees of the Garden of Eden. Abraham's first act in Be'er Sheva, after he signed his peace treaty with the King of the Philistines, was to plant a tamarisk tree. He thus provided shade and hospitality for weary travelers to comfortably discuss monotheism. Jacob instructed his children to plant acacia trees due to his foresight that the Jews would need to build a *Mishkan*, a portable sanctuary, as they wandered the desert for forty years. The Baal Shem Tov, the great founder of the Chasidic Movement, learned to talk to the trees, plants, and animals in the forests of Eastern Europe as a child. Rabbi Nachman, a *tzaddik gadol*, a righteous man of his generation, recommended going outdoors each day among the trees to pray in solitude and experience the oneness and preciousness of creation.

The Talmud tells the oft-repeated tale of the sage Choni walking along a road. He saw an old man planting a carob tree. Choni asked him, "How long will it take for this tree to bear fruit?"

"Seventy years," replied the man.

Choni then asked: "Are you so healthy a man that you expect to live that length of time and eat its fruit?"

The man answered, "I found a fruitful world because my ancestors planted it for me. Likewise, I am planting for my children."

I wonder if Eon and his sister Elin will remember the Spring sleepover when they first planted trees in Eon's Forest. The night before, I told them that we could do some gardening the next morning. Eon, age three, remembered when he helped plant the pea, radish, and beet seeds a month earlier. Elin, age one-and-a-half, had busied herself putting some landscaping rocks in a bucket of water.

After breakfast, Eon was so enthusiastic about going outside that, in his haste, he initially put his boots on the wrong feet. Grandma Donna got Elin's little shoes on and put her in the stroller. I grabbed my two biggest cedar tree saplings, a CobraHead weeder for digging, and a little spade for Eon to use. Eon carried the spade.

Eon got to pick the spot on the rough ground to plant his tree. A CobraHead weeder can easily dig the hole for a sapling and clear a little circle of weeds when the ground is nice and soft. I did most of the digging. Eon got to place the sapling in the hole and push the dirt back in. He got to hold the hose as we watered in our new, little, green cedar tree.

The next seedling to plant was Elin's tree. She said, "no," when asked if she wanted to get out of her stroller and plant a tree, but she carefully watched us plant her tree. Eon also told her, "This is your tree, baby!" With his hands, Eon helped move the dirt that I dug with the CobraHead weeding tool. After positioning the tree just right, the same little hands went to work to help fill the hole back in and pat down the dirt. This time, we made a little earthen moat around the new planting as the ground there sloped a bit. We wanted to make sure the rainwater didn't run off so that Elin's tree got a good soak when it rained.

When the kids visit, they are happy to walk outside to see Eon's Forest. We have now planted a total of five cedar trees, one pine tree, one fir tree, and one bush. I am sure their parents have already instilled in these children a love of trees from their many nature walks and frequent visits to the parks near their house. Children naturally love playing and walking around outside. They will likely grow up to be environmentalists, a value their parents have already clearly instilled in them, and that has grown out of many family activities.

Our earnest hope as grandparents is that long after we are "pushing up daisies," that Eon's Forest trees will continue to grow big and strong, like Eon and Elin. Whether or not Eon and Elin remember their adventures planting trees with Grandma Donna and me, the trees of Eon's Forest will do what trees were meant to do, dating back to the time of creation and Adam and Eve—contribute to the health of the planet and human beings everywhere.

The earth's deforestation that continues to result from fires, agricultural practices, urban expansion, and excessive logging is a worldwide threat to our children and grandchildren. We all need to cultivate and guard our trees and forests and recognize they form part of our source of life. I like to think of our forests as the lungs of the earth. Perhaps one day, planting trees with children and grandchildren will help bring back the biodiversity needed to transform our world into the abundant and beneficent Garden it was meant to be.

IDEAS

- *Give a tree as a gift to your grandkids.*

- *Plant a tree in memory of a loved one.*

- *Tell your grandchild about your favorite tree.*

- *Picnic with your grandchildren in the shade of a special tree.*

BLESSINGS

(Completing Our Life Cycle)

"The memory of the righteous is invoked in blessing,"
but "the fame of the wicked rots."

PROVERBS 10:7

My dad always subscribed to two daily newspapers, one delivered in the morning and the other in the afternoon. He dutifully read the obituaries of each every day. These days, I learn of a friend or colleague's passing from a post on social media far more often than from an obituary or phone call. After I turned sixty, I started noticing that more friends and colleagues were dying, and the pace picked up as I turned the corner into my seventies. If I had no clue the person had been ill, the notice of their passing might hit me like a ton of bricks. But even if the death followed a lot of suffering from health problems of which I had been aware, the news invariably causes an instant and serious pause, a reflection, an acknowledgment, and a desire to share the news with my wife, my kids, or a friend. The knowledge permeates my consciousness for a time and sometimes for days or months. I don't like going to funerals or memorial celebrations, but sometimes I feel compelled to go, even if attending doesn't do much for me. While the pace of these notices and memorials quickens in this decade of my life, the sequela of feelings is not ameliorated. I don't feel calloused by the experiences. I remember the adage my mother employed when she was elderly. She used to say that you need courage to grow old.

Jews like to say, "May her memory be a blessing." This refers to the nice things we remember about the deceased—the positive attributes of her personality, her good deeds, how she lived, and what she taught us from her example. The saying conveys a warmth and caring that is also intended to comfort the mourner. Remembering a parent or grandparent to whom you were particularly close oftentimes brings a flood of feelings.

I remember sobbing at my grandmother's funeral service. What triggered my breakdown happened at the end of the speechifying, most of which I don't remember. The rabbi opened it up to the assemblage packed into the little memorial chapel to stand and share a few words. My grandmother was very popular and hosted many family and social gatherings, including what my mom called her culture group. She played piano and sang, primarily, but not exclusively, Yiddish and operatic or show-tune music with a small circle of amateur singers and musicians. At her funeral service, one of the regulars of the culture group, who I remembered well but had not seen in years, stood up and slowly opened his violin case. Bent over and clearly not the maestro on the instrument he once was, he played a few bars of a Yiddish tune that evoked his sadness for the loss of my grandmother. That opened the floodgates for me. After the service concluded, and almost everyone had filed out to the foyer, I was still seated in my chair, sobbing away.

Perhaps witnessing that moment is why my mother told me in her later years, "Andy, don't geschrei (cry) and carry on for me when I'm gone. I had a good life, and I don't want you to feel bad."

She understood the buried depth of my feelings, and she didn't want me to suffer. The only thing I remember telling my kids about my demise is, if there's a funeral, keep it short. In the meantime, I haven't lived my life ever thinking about what anyone might or might not say about me when it's time for a eulogy or an obituary.

I do worry about the degree to which I may cling to life, if conscious, in my dying days. Some people imagine death as reuniting with family, reincarnating, or entering a realm of nothingness. I don't know what to think, other than experiencing a fear of a final unknown.

I can admire what the Baal Shem Tov told his disciples as death closed in. He said, "Until now, I have acted with loving-kindness toward you; now it is time for you to reciprocate." I lack confidence that I can copy his example, and I don't have any followers to gather close. I'm not on his level, not even close.

I would like it, however, if I could provide a kindness and bless my children and grandchildren in my final days—moments akin to the Patriarch Jacob, who blessed Joseph and his sons while on his deathbed. I fear choking up or breaking down, as I did at my grandmother's funeral, and not being able to depart with kindness to those who I care about most.

In the Book of Genesis, Joseph brought his sons, Manasseh and Ephriam, to visit and honor his father, Jacob, in Jacob's final days. The emotional scene is described in Genesis (48:11), "'I never even hoped to see your face,' said Israel [Jacob] to Joseph. 'But now God has even let me see your children.'" (48:11)

Jacob blessed Joseph, and then he blessed his grandsons, "[In time to come] Israel will use you as a blessing. They will say, 'May God make you like Ephriam and Manasseh.'"

This blessing has, in fact, been repeated in the Sabbath liturgy for centuries.

Jewish sages and commentators explain the beauty of blessing your grandchildren. Parents naturally worry about their children, who frequently rebel against their parents. In other words, children and their parents, especially during the teenage years, often experience rocky or tempestuous times in their relationships. The grandparent relationship usually isn't like that. The grandparent relationship is much more likely to be freer, more relaxed, and untroubled by anywhere near as much tension or anxiety. Although we say as parents that we love our children unconditionally, the love of a grandparent of the grandchild is a truer example. Thus, Jacob's blessing, a loving expression towards his grandchildren, became a model spanning generations.

Time spent with grandchildren is a learning opportunity for the kids, but also for the grandparents. While grandparents bless their grandchildren, anyone who has enjoyed having grandchildren knows that grandparents are blessed by them. Perhaps that's why the Sabbath liturgy also ends with the famous words of Psalm 128:6, "May you live to see your children's children—peace be on Israel."

As the great Jewish sages point out, caring about grandchildren means caring about the future. Those who think about the future, it follows, yearn for peace. Those who make war are those who focus on their past anger and seek revenge.

I am so sorry that, as I near the finish line, my grandchildren are likely to face a world of violence, environmental degradation, and upheaval. All the more reason to bless them now and in the time I have left.

I've often wondered, and previously written, if humanity succumbed to its current predicament, after being born into a perfect world, what's to stop us from traveling in the opposite direction, heavenward, while here on earth? Maybe, just maybe, we can commence the redemption of humanity by giving our grandchildren our very best. Who knows what blessings they will bring?

THINK ABOUT

- *How did you experience the loss of your grandparents?*

RESOURCES

See, "Be Honest and Concrete: Tips For Talking To Kids About Death," by Anya Kamenetz and Cory Turner, *See*, https://www.wbur.org/npr/716702066/death-talking-with-kids-about-the-end

ACKNOWLEDGMENTS

Abigail Drapkin is an extraordinary artist. She jump-started my writing career when she illustrated my first book, *The Spiritual Gardener*, surrounding my words with watercolors that conveyed elegance and grace. Thank you, Abigail, for collaborating again on my grandparenting book with your beautiful illustrations.

Very special thanks to beta readers Ben Zion Hershberg, Marion Schwartz, and Giovanna Franklin, whose suggestions and eagle eyes immeasurably improved this book's quality.

Additionally, Giovanna Franklin and her husband, Steve Franklin, have again supported my writing by sponsoring this book for which I am very grateful.

Lastly, this is my third book working with Howard VanEs and his wonderful team at Let's Write Books. Howard, your talents, advice, and friendship are deeply appreciated.

FROM OUR SPONSOR

"La familia è uno dei capolavori della natura."

Translated from Italian:

"The family is one of nature's masterpieces."

We are proud to support this endearing tribute to family, with a spotlight on the unique bond between grandparents and grandchildren. Overflowing with nostalgia and tender unforgettable moments, Andy's ("Grandy's") personal experiences, spiritual reflections, and practical considerations are sure to warm the heart and inspire. It is a must-read for anyone who cherishes the special connection between grandparents and their grandchildren.

- Steve & Giovanna Franklin

ABOUT THE ARTIST

Abigail Drapkin is a painter and printmaker from Maine. She holds an MFA in painting and drawing from the University of Washington and a BA in studio art from Brandeis University. She lives in Seattle, where she teaches painting, drawing, and printmaking classes to adults, college students, and youth through the Gage Academy of Art, the University of Washington, and the Lake Washington Institute of Technology. Ms. Drapkin has exhibited her oil paintings and prints in group shows and solo showcases in San Francisco, Seattle, Singapore, and France.

ABOUT THE AUTHOR

Andy Becker is a writer, gardener, and lifetime learner who lives in Western Washington among the cedar trees with his wife, Donna, and their two dogs, Nova and Splash. Andy was a successful small-town lawyer who found respite from the vicissitudes of fighting for the little guy against insurance companies by gardening, hiking, and camping with his family, and by expanding his spirituality through Judaism. Andy's writing has been directly fueled by his lifetime experiences and influenced by Chassidic philosophy.

His *Spiritual Garden Series* consists of three books that each contain elements of memoir: *The Spiritual Gardener*, *The Spiritual Forest*, and *Grandy, Let's Play!* The series begins with *The Spiritual Gardner*, describing the spiritual rewards and just plain fun of digging in the dirt to grow vegetables. *The Spiritual Forest* describes the importance of trees, forests, and environmentalism; in other words, the spiritual value of caring for and growing trees. The series is capped off with the joy and blessings of family and growing grandchildren in *Grandy, Let's Play!*

Andy's other books include *Cracking an Egg*, funny, early childhood vignettes that he wrote as a love letter to his mom, and *The Kissing Rabbi*, an award-winning novel inspired by an actual *#MeToo* scandal that rocked the Tacoma community. There, the novel's narrator channels his inner Sholem Aleichem to address themes of lust, betrayal, polarization, and viral news with humor and satire.

Andy has given multiple presentations in person (and on Zoom) at bookstores, Jewish Community Centers, Synagogues, Senior Centers, Nurseries, Gardening Clubs, and Service Groups. He is an active member of a local non-profit writer's group.

The Spiritual Gardener won the New York City Big Book Award in the Home and Garden category.

The Kissing Rabbi won a First Place Chanticleer Mark Twain Award for Humor and Satire.

The Spiritual Forest was a Finalist in the National Indie Excellence Awards, Indie Book Awards, and the Best Book Awards in the categories of Spirituality and Nature.

Presently, Andy's time is devoted to writing, gardening, planting trees, supporting environmentalism, and most enjoyably, spending time with his family, and especially his grandchildren.

www.ingramcontent.com/pod-product-compliance
Lightning Source LLC
Chambersburg PA
CBHW060539100426
42742CB00013B/2393